BOGORODITSK

TAGANROG

ZINCIRLI

BAGHDAD

DARABJERD

GUR

M

NAHALAL

MARE INDICVM

E V
A

Cities in the Round

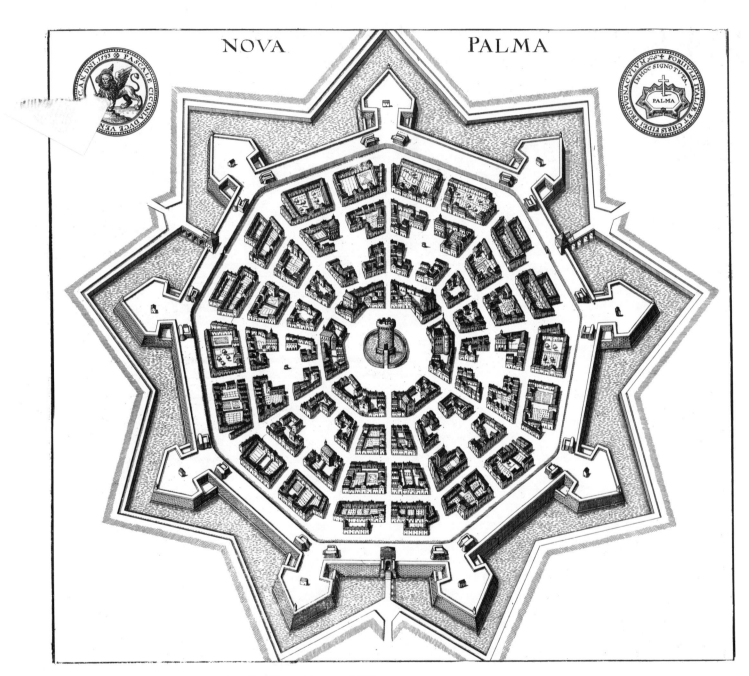

NOVA PALMA

Plan of Palmanova (engraving by Matthaeus Merian, 1650)

CITIES IN THE ROUND

Norman J. Johnston

UNIVERSITY OF WASHINGTON PRESS   *Seattle & London*

Library of Congress Cataloging in Publication Data

Johnston, Norman J.
    Cities in the round.

    Bibliography: p.
    Includes index.
    1. City planning—History. I. Title.
NA9090.J6   711'.41   81-21984
ISBN 0-295-95918-5   AACR2

This book was published with the assistance of a grant from the National
Endowment for the Humanities.

Endpaper maps were drawn by the author.

To Janie

Preface

ALTHOUGH there have been many cities whose natural growth processes gave them variously circular plans, history offers only a scattering of the *planned* circular city. More frequent in theoretical literature than in reality, it has an arbitrary quality that is likely to repel the modern observer and discourage its use. Yet in spite of what to us may appear to be its obvious shortcomings, the surprise is that the planned circular city is not only a venerable member of the family of urban forms but has stubbornly persisted in urban speculations and applications even to this day. In it there is the suggestion of an environmental language that goes beyond the rational, employing a vocabulary that is emotional, collective, and archetypal. For this reason alone, the planned circular city deserves to have a book devoted to it.

Even the patterns of circular cities are feast enough for the senses to merit their being brought together for our pleasure. Lewis Mumford couples language and the city as humanity's greatest works of art; surely the planned circular city is the most ambitious effort to give that art its ultimate formal expression. Its plans dazzle the eye even though they may leave a residue of doubt as to their practical applications. Perhaps what is needed is the admonition to avoid an overly judgmental attitude toward the phenomenon. Instead, enjoy these cities for the purity of their concept, the ambitions of their builders, and the variety of their interpretations.

For convenience, the term "planned circular city" is rather broadly used here to include polygonal and concentric variants. Thus, by "planned circular city" I mean planned cities of five or more sides symmetrically arranged about a central point. In this I claim a distinguished precedent: Leone Battista Alberti assigned the highest order of beauty to the circular form but recognized a hierarchy of centrally-planned polygons of a decreasing number of sides that descend from that ultimate.

My pursuit of the pleasures of circular cities has been spread over a number of years, tracing them in the literature and through visits to most of the existing sites and all of the classic examples of the genre. In this I have been assisted by grants from the Research Fund of the College of Architecture and Urban Planning and by the Graduate School Research Fund, both at the University of Washington, and by my sabbatical year from the university in 1976–77 which gave me the luxury of time sufficient to include extended travel. Nor would I want to go unnoted the support and presence of my wife during these years: her faith in the validity of the effort and its ultimate publication but also her patient sharing with me of visits to my circular cities when there was every likelihood she would have preferred the time in more glamorous settings.

The literature of the planned circular city is drawn from many sources; those I used are listed in the bibliography and acnowledged in the text. I want, however, to recognize especially my indebtedness to the late E. A. Gutkind and his *International History of City Development*. I was privileged to study with Dr. Gutkind and to assist in the preparation of one of his volumes. The comprehensiveness of his coverage of the general topic made it inevitable that I would turn to his *Interna-*

tional History in developing my more specialized study.

Various associates have made possible the fitting together of the pieces that are required to build a study such as this. My University of Washington colleague John Rohrer drew a handsome series of panoramic city views, and another colleague, Astra Zarina, and her husband Tony Heywood introduced me to new material which added to my resources. Important contributions in shaping the book were made by others of my university associates who read the manuscript, offered valuable suggestions, and helped me to avoid some of the seductions of my own words: Grant Hildebrand, John L. Hancock, Marga Rose Hancock, and Thomas L. Bosworth. Donald H. Miller's interest included his giving a print to my collection of original circular city engravings. Because this book draws from a range of languages, my translators have been especially helpful at key points in my investigations: Charity Small, Hermann Pundt, Richard Ludwig, Jay Reinhardt, Genevra Gerhardt, the Jan Diepenheims, Anna White, and Renata Morte. Mary Davies was patient with changes in copy even after she thought she had completed a final typing. To each of those mentioned above, I am grateful for efforts that often combined scholarship with generous acts of friendship.

Contents

    I. Circles: The Persistent Symbol   3

   II. Circular Cities of the Ancient Near East   13

  III. The Classical World's Circular City Theories   21

  IV. The Circular City of the Medieval World   26

   V. Renaissance Circular Cities: Fifteenth and Sixteenth Centuries   31

  VI. Baroque Circular Cities: Seventeenth and Eighteenth Centuries   62

 VII. Circular Cities of the Nineteenth and Twentieth Centuries   102

VIII. A Postscript for Circular Cities   126

      Notes   129

      Bibliography   133

      Index   137

Illustrations

Plan of Palmanova *Frontispiece*
1. Plan of Zulu settlement 4
2. Plan of Bororo village 5
3. Plan of Krahno Indian village 5
4. Plan of Stonehenge 6
5. Ancient and traditional circular symbols 7
6. Medieval paving maze 8
7. Yin and yang disc 8
8. Indian mandala 9
9. Egyptian hieroglyph for "city" 10
10. Plan of Zincirli 14
11. Nimrud bas-relief 15
12. Plan of Darabjerd 16
13. Gur 17
14. Plan of Baghdad 18
15. Plan of Mantinea 23
16. Vitruvian town plan diagram 25
17. Plan of Nördlingen 26
18. Plan of Bram 27
19. Plan of Eketorp 27
20. Jerusalem 28
21. Mexcaltitán 29
22. Renaissance perspective 33
23. Vitruvian figure 34
24. Centrally-planned circular church 35
25. Cataneo, circular church plan 35
26. Filarete, plan of Sforzinda 37
27. Martini, ideal cities 38
28. Giocondo, ideal city 39
29. Cataneo, ideal cities 40

30. Scamozzi, ideal city 41
31. Speckle, ideal city 42
32. Fortifications glossary 43
33. Marchi, fortress 44
34. Plan of Marienbourg, 1649 46
35. Plan of Philippeville, 1710 47
36. Plan of Nové Zámky, 1595 48
37. Zuerius van Boxhorn, plan of Willemstad, 1632 49
38. Willemstad 51
39. Plan of Coevorden 52
40. Plan of Vitry-le-François 53
41. Plan of Villefranche-sur-Meuse, 1650 54
42. Plan of Rocroi, 1650 55
43. Schickhardt, plan of Freudenstadt, c. 1600 55
44. Plan of Palmanova 57
45. Plan of Palmanova, 1851 58
46. Palmanova 60
47. Military engineering for an eighteenth-century fortress city 63
48. Eighteenth-century military engineering 65
49. Sardi, ideal city 66
50. Dilich, ideal cities 67
51. Rimpler, ideal city 68
52. Perret, ideal cities 69
53. Errard de Bar-le-Duc, ideal cities 71
54. Vauban's fortifications for Lille 72
55. An eighteenth-century English romantic landscape 74
56. Plan of Scherpenheuvel, 1660 76
57. Plan of Henrichemont, 1608 76
58. Plan of Charleroi 77
59. Plan of Vauban's Longwy fortifications 78

60. Plan of Saarlouis, 1713   79
61. Plan of Neuf Brisach, c. 1710   80
62. Neuf Brisach   82
63. Plan of Santo Stefano di Camastra with modern extensions   84
64. Plan of Avola, 1756   85
65. Grammichele's evolution   86
66. Engraving of Karlsruhe, 1739   89
67. Plan of Leopoldov, seventeenth century   90
68. Le Blond, plan for St. Petersburg, 1717   91
69. Plans of late eighteenth-century Russian fortress cities   92
70. Plan of Taganrog, late eighteenth century   93
71. Plan of Bogoroditsk, 1778   94
72. Various eighteenth-century Russian semicircular cities   95
73. Plan of Hamina, c. 1750   96
74. Hamina   97
75. View of Chaux   99
76. Ledoux, plan of Chaux   101
77. Pemberton, plan for Queen Victoria town, 1854   104
78. Howard, Garden City diagrams   105
79. Gloeden, circular cities regional plan, 1923   106

80. Gloeden, plan of a circular city, 1923   106
81. Wolf, diagram for a circular city, 1919   107
82. Soleri, plan of a circular city, 1969   108
83. Nineteenth-century French casino cities   109
84. Plan of Latina, c. 1940   110
85. Nahalal   111
86. Plan of Whiteley Village   112
87. The squaring of Circleville   113
88. Clubb, plan for an octagonal city   114
89. Allen, plan for an octagonal block and city, 1873   115
90. Plan of Almondale   116
91. Plan of Cotati   117
92. Cotati   118
93. Cooke, plan for Llano, 1915   119
94. Austin, plan for Llano, c. 1916   119
95. Plan of Boa Vista   120
96. View of Urubupunga   121
97. Roberto plan for Brasilia   122
98. Urban unit in Roberto plan for Brasilia   124
99. Partial plan of Sun City   125

Cities in the Round

With the straight ruler I set to work to inscribe a square within this circle; in its center will be the marketplace, into which all the straight streets lead, converging to this center like a star, which, although only circular, sends forth its rays in a straight line from all sides.

Aristophanes, *The Birds* (414 B.C.)

I. Circles: The Persistent Symbol

CITIES PLANNED in the round whose symmetrical patterns of form and space are a marriage of mathematics and art: to twentieth-century city residents more conscious of urban disorder and visual confusion, such visions of the city must appear as ephemeral as the snow crystals they so often resemble. Yet they have a curious persistence in the history of cities. At least in those parts of the world thought of as sharing in the Western tradition, these circular cities are found among our early urban efforts, and variations on the theme have continued into our own times. Few such cities were actually built, but as a planning approach the concept was reinterpreted and reapplied in a variety of contexts over many years, testifying to an attraction that transcends mere coincidence. Arbitrary as they may seem to us, the circular plan and its mutations prove to have had an engaging presence through much of urban history.

Cities with circular plans are part of a wider universe sharing the same symbolic language. There is a considerable literature on the meaning of symbols and their relation to the nature and motivations of the human personality. Carl Jung and a group of his colleagues have thoroughly explored the phenomenon and clarified the extent to which symbols are themselves expressive of more than immediate appearances. In *Man and His Symbols* they note that

. . . a symbol always stands for something more than its obvious and immediate meaning. . . . There are many symbols . . . that are not individual but *collective* in their nature and origin . . . they are in fact "collective representations," emanating from primeval

dreams and creative fantasies. As such, these images are involuntary spontaneous manifestations and by no means intentional inventions.[1]

Peter Smith reinforces these observations with speculations about how symbols are engrammed, or registered in one's memory, over time and by repetition so as to ensure for them "a permanent part of the mesocortical circuitry" by their cultural persistence.[2] Such writers clarify the role played by symbols in human activity and the extent to which they reflect unconscious and archaic origins within the human psyche, even when applied to such pragmatic concerns as the plan of a city.

In the hierarchical structure of this symbolic language, conscious and unconscious, the circle is located in the uppermost ranks. Among ancient peoples and modern, literate or primitive, East or West, the circle is employed by all and assigned meanings with a shared consistency. Perfection, wholeness, harmony: whether in the individual, the godhead, or the universe, the circle is found to represent these attainments. The natural world offers numerous reminders of circular forms: the sun and moon, the imprint of a raindrop on water's surface, the blossoms and seeds of certain plants. Nature's movements are often circular as well: the days, the seasons, the years, even the rhythm of life itself. As Nader Ardalan and Laleh Bakhtiar observe:

The heavens are said to move in a circular motion because such a form has no beginning and no end and is symmetrical in all directions with respect to the center. The circle is instrumental in the conception of man who, in the microcosm, begins life as a sphere, perceives the visual world through the spheres of his eyes, and completes a full circle upon his death.[3]

Bruno Munari notes spontaneous human actions that also reaffirm circularity: a child's early drawing; the circle formed when people are attracted about something to observe it; the circle of the dance, "no one is first, no one is last—all are equal and all stamp alike."[4] Or consider the language: our "circle of friends," our "inner circle."

Something of this spontaneity, in due course reinforced by long-standing tradition and ancestral approbation, can be found in the village patterns of primitive societies. Drawing in varying degrees from religious, defensive, and societal concerns, various peoples have used the circle to satisfy their planning needs and give structure to their settlements and lives. The royal Zulu cities of the nineteenth century, whose circular plans were rooted in primitive protective stockades for home and cattle (fig. 1), adapted and extended this kraal module to enormous dimensions. Barrie Biermann has called them "the most persuasive demonstration of the generic powers of an elementary geometrical principle consistently applied as a design theme."[5] One such is described by a contemporary observer as being nearly a mile in diameter, with the king's kraal at the center while "the huts of the warriors and their families . . . are placed in four- or even five-fold ranks; so that the kraal almost rises to the dignity of a town, having several thousand inhabitants, and presenting a singularly imposing appearance when viewed at a distance."[6]

Brazil offers similar evidence of circular settlements. The Bororo of Mato Grosso not only planned their villages with strict cardinal-point orientation, encircling the men's house and dance platform, but their subdivision and spatial assign-

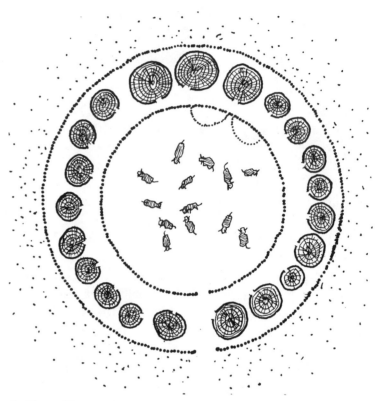

1. *Plan of Zulu settlement*

ments were also a means for governing the tribal and class structure of the village (fig. 2).

The Salesian missionaries who first dealt with [the Bororo] found that the only way to approach them was to persuade them to leave their traditional village and settle in a new village of rectangular huts set out in parallel rows. This completely destroyed the complex Bororo social system which was so closely tied to the layout of the village that it could not survive transplantation into a different environment. . . . [The Bororo] felt completely disorientated in the world, once

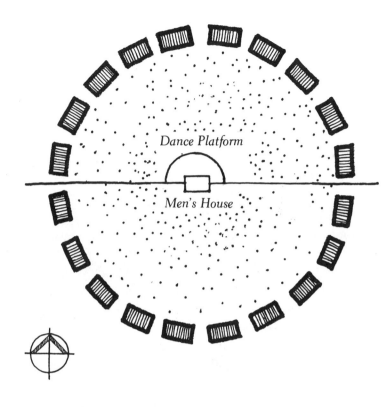

formed a giant "C" opening to the east and the rising sun. Tradition further determined tribal location within the tented perimeter, certain positions carrying more status than others. The center remained open except for the tents of the great council and the meetings of the forty-four peace chiefs. These camp circles were a widely practiced custom among many American Plains Indians.[8]

Ancient scientific attention was also focused on the circle. Assyrians, Babylonians, Egyptians, Phoenicians, Greeks—all were fascinated by its characteristics and tried to rationalize them. Babylon gave us its 360 degrees, based on the 360-day

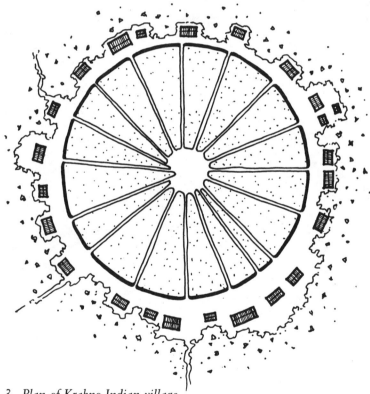

2. Plan of Bororo village

they were divorced from the traditional cosmology demonstrated in the village plan.[7] [Joseph Rykwert]

There still continue to be Amazonian tribes such as the Krahno Indians living in villages whose plans resemble great wheels, with spokes radiating out from the center to a hut-lined rim (fig. 3).

Even such nomadic people as the Cheyennes of the American Plains chose a circular arrangement when they met for temporary tribal assemblies. As many as a thousand tents

3. Plan of Krahno Indian village

year and the assigned distance the sun traveled each day to complete its progress. Trigonometry was the result of Ptolemaic efforts to understand the planets and calculate their movements.[9] For all these early peoples, mathematics' most venerable preoccupation continued to be efforts to square the circle (an impossible mission, though one that the Egyptians, among the ancients, came closest to completing).

Another people's understanding of the characteristics of the circle and of cosmic order is becoming increasingly appreciated with modern analysis of Britain's Stonehenge (fig. 4). This famous Bronze Age sanctuary (along with a similar and larger

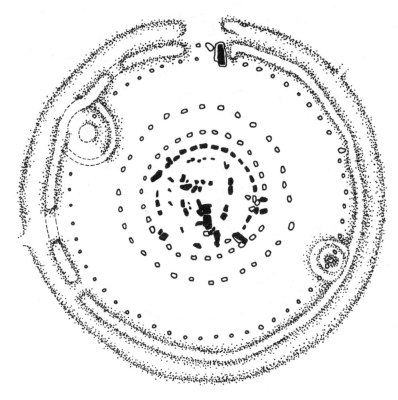

4. *Plan of Stonehenge*

stone monument at Avebury), although never intended for settlement purposes, nevertheless reaffirms the ubiquitous fascination of the circle and its properties, coupled with the shared human search for order and position in a universe of troubling uncertainties.

But the circle's power to enlist the human imagination lies less in its rational principles than in its symbolic potentials. Here its timeless versatility unfolds, affirmed in a variety of evidence that can be found in the symbolic language of peoples widely separated in both time and space. To the Jungian psychoanalysts, the circle is a visual symbol of the self, an expression of human self-fulfillment and search for wholeness. For those of the Zen sect, the circle combines human perfection and enlightenment.[10] From ancient times the no-beginning, no-end nature of the circle lent itself to symbolic associations with eternity, the divine, with heaven, with the sleeping eye of God. "God is a circle whose center is everywhere, but whose circumference is nowhere."[11] The god Brahma makes his survey in preparation for the creation by standing at the center of a circle, a thousand-petaled lotus blossom. A story relates similar events in which Buddha assumes the central role. Both gods, in spatially orienting themselves to their task, affirm symbolically "the human need for psychic orientation."[12]

In symbolic language, the circle finds widespread and versatile expression. Much of the linguistic work toward establishing a written language, prehistoric to modern, employed it as a basic element. But a similar versatility appears in its uses for religious, mythic, and magic purposes, even more revealing of the status that it occupied in symbolic hierarchies. Rudolf Koch has examined in some detail a full range of "signs" used from earliest times through the Middle Ages and has identified 493 of them. Of that number, 62 are based on the circle or have designs fundamentally derived from its presence as part of the symbol. Thus, as seen in figure 5, such signs include: the

God, eternity, fire

Open eye of God, sun, air

Water, salt, female element

Sun, earth

Jesus Christ

Orb of earth and water, universe

5. *Ancient and traditional circular symbols*

circle with a dot at the center—the open eye of God (also the astronomical sign for the sun, the sign for air, and the botanical sign for annual); the circle divided vertically—"And God divided the light from the darkness," the male element, what comes from on high; the circle divided horizontally—"And God divided the waters which were under the firmament from the waters which were above the firmament," the passive female element, what has been there from the beginning of all things, water, salt; two consecutive circles about a dark center—the universe, the orb of the earth and water, the work with its rings of atmosphere and heaven.

The circle is especially pervasive in the symbolism of the medieval church. The creation is the joining of the male and female symbols as one (even earlier this was the sun of northern mythology and of the ancient East). The ancient pagan sun wheel became for Christianity the representation of Jesus (I) and Christ (X). The circle with double cross combines the Christian cross and Greek X; with two circles we have added the inner eternity, the outer finite. The four elements of medieval mysticism also are assigned symbolic identity employing the circle: air, earth, fire, and water.[13] For St. Augustine, one of the Latin fathers of the church and founder of theology, the circle in his doctrine was manifestation of purest form.

Certain other uses remind us of the attraction the European medieval world felt toward symbolism in general and the circle in particular: the circular mazes and labyrinths of medieval gardens, pavings, and manuscripts (fig. 6); the halos of Christ and the saints; the great rose windows of the cathedrals; and even King Arthur's legendary court with his knights assembled about the round table as a reminder of their equality.

From the East there comes an especially rich history of circular symbolism. One of the oldest expressions, the yin and yang disk, is perhaps the most familiar, with its representation of the balance of opposite forces within the universe (fig. 7).

6. *Medieval paving maze*

A literal description of a mandala is that it is a graphic mystic symbol of the universe or cosmos, usually circular in outline, typically with a symmetrical arrangement of forms and patterns representing the deities. These physical properties emphasize the *center*, not only of the mandala itself but also as reference to the beginning point of all other forms and processes. *"In the Beginning was the Center,"* write the authors of *Mandala*, "the center of the mind of God, the eternal Creator, the Dream of Brahman, the galaxies that swirl beyond the lenses of our great telescopes. In all of these the center is one, and in the center lies eternity."[14] Concentric levels move out from that center, suggesting a succession of passages, with the

7. *Yin and yang disk*

But the complex and visually evocative patterns of mandalas provide the largest body of evidence of the role the circle played in the Eastern world (fig. 8). Here we are dealing with those aspects that emphasize the circle's perfection, wholeness, and harmony. It draws the individual into the process of self-contemplation, self-discovery, the universal search whose relevance is timely and timeless through all ages and among all peoples. Although the mandala form is not unique to Eastern practices (England's Stonehenge or a medieval rose window are variations on the theme), its presence, especially in the art and imagery of Buddhism and Hinduism, is notable.

8. Indian mandala

circle representing the heavens containing the square of the earth which they enclose.

But the mandala's physical properties are accessory to a more profound and complex purpose—an aid to meditation.

The healing, meditative, integrative purpose of the Mandala has its beginning and its root in man's attempt at self-orientation. Man is the center of his own relative time/space locus from which he receives a cosmic consecration. Whatever is in front, behind, to the left, and right of him become the four cardinal directions; whatever is above and below become the heavens and the earth; what was yesterday and will be tomorrow becomes time past and time future—and the center is always the individual, the bearer of the awareness of the eternal *now*.[15] [José and Miriam Argüelles]

Through the mandala tradition India, China, and especially Tibet have given rich affirmation to the visual and psychic potentials of the circle and its special meaning as symbol in expressing processes and values central to human concerns.

Similar mandala-like approaches to such concerns are found elsewhere as well. The eight-petaled solar flowers of Hawaii, the great altar stones of the Aztecs, the medicine wheels of the Indians of the American Southwest, even the tradition of magic circles and Mennonite hex signs: all are forms and values that remind us of a shared humanity and efforts of diverse peoples to employ a vocabulary of symbols that will assist them in securing their place in a mysterious universe.

But of all the applications of the mystic circle to human concerns, the most physically audacious are those that involve the shaping of the human environment and most especially the city. There is an understandable coincidence here, since both architecture and the city had origins that transcended mere utilitarian shelter and community. The nature of present-day society and values tends to obscure these origins and the extent to which they were formed initially out of sacred circumstances attended by appropriate religious rituals. These reflected again a search for a cosmic order of events, a rationale in which human efforts and daily life found a comforting and protected place. The hearth, the tribal shrine, the ceremonial complex—from the simplest of environmental beginnings to the most elaborate they were all seen as requiring a continuity with the supernatural and the mystic. The environment, by its honoring of a higher and celestial order, would secure for its occupants a place in that order and inclusion under the protection of a heavenly and eternal godly presence. Rulers were God's representatives; the cosmic city on earth was a *Civitas Dei*.

What better security for such objectives than to employ the sacred circle, the mandala or its permutations, as prototype plan, "to build a world through art that reflects equilibrium, serenity, and peace"?[16] Doing so transcends utilitarian objectives, though these may not necessarily be violated. Thus, a circular wall drawn around the city lends itself to a system of defense, but in those cases where "ideal objectives" were most self-consciously sought in the city's plan, defensive benefits were welcome but coincidental. Under such circumstances, esthetics were also incidental to the primacy of sacred order. Eventually, utilitarian or esthetic secular objectives assumed more conscious priority. But the roots of the matter—even in those later, less incorporeal times—would still lie, according to the Jungians, at primordial levels:

Whether in classical or in primitive foundations, the mandala ground plan was never dictated by considerations of aesthetics or economics. It was a transformation of the city into an ordered cosmos, a sacred place bound by its center to the other world. And this transformation accorded with the vital feelings and needs of religious man.

Every building, sacred or secular, that has a mandala ground plan is the projection of an archetypal image from within the human unconscious onto the outer world. The city, the fortress, and the temple become symbols of psychic wholeness, and in this way exercise a specific influence on the human being who enters or lives in the place. (It need hardly be emphasized that even in architecture the projection of the psychic content was a purely unconscious process. "Such things cannot be thought up," Dr. Jung has written, "but must grow again from the forgotten depths if they are to express the deepest insights of consciousness and the loftiest intuitions of the spirit, thus amalgamating the uniqueness of present-day conscious-

ness with the age-old past of humanity.")[17]

So we have the city's plan as an expression, both conscious and unconscious, of a sacred order. Such motivations did not exclude plan forms other than the circle; the square, the rectangle, and polygons could be similarly employed. All are members of the same family of geometry, but within that family the circle has a primacy; unlike the other members with their progression of identified number of sides, the circle is a figure with an infinite number of sides. Even the language reinforces its urban precedence: the oldest writing that we are able to read, Egyptian hieroglyphics, offers for "city" a circle enclosing a cross (fig. 9).

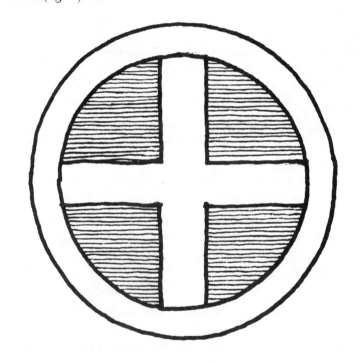

9. *Egyptian hieroglyph for "city"*

In the acceptance of the circle as the plan form for idealized cosmic cities, however, there was to be a break between the Eastern and Western worlds. Whereas in the West it was a characteristic theoretical device and was occasionally realized, for the East a different application of the mandala concept was employed. The Eastern mandala combines two sacred elements within its context, the circle and the square, with each assigned a different symbolic task. The circle is a representation of the heavens while the square is that of the earth. This is established with most clarity in Chinese practice and is rigorously reflective of their interpretation of the universe. For the ancient Chinese, as for the Western world, the heavens were round and celestially ordered. The earth, however, was conceived by the Chinese as a square, an artificial human world, whereas in the ancient West it was always circular. This concept has literal consequences in Chinese environmental design: e.g., the circular Altar of Heaven and the square Altar of Earth, or the square platform of a Buddhist stupa with a superimposed circular dome.[18]

It follows then that the Chinese with their ancient ritualistic observances attending the building of cities would acknowledge their earthbound nature and human roots by decisions affecting urban design. From as early as the fifth century B.C. the evidence suggests that the Chinese did identify city design with their view of the earth as square or rectangular in shape and ritualistically oriented to the four cardinal compass points. Furthermore (an additional affirmation of China's traditional ethnocentricity) their imperial capital was viewed as being at the earth's center, surrounded by successive rectangular zones of decreasing degrees of civilization which ended in a final outer zone of "cultureless savagery."

The planning of the Chinese city with its patterns, forms, and spaces was a reflection of this view of the cosmos. Subscribing to its earthbound nature with appropriate orthography and compass-point orientation, the city was thereby enfolded into the all-encompassing system of the cosmos. It was a reflection of locational priorities in which the position of the imperial palace took precedence, followed by a succession of rankings in which all other aspects of Chinese life found their appropriate hierarchical position.[19]

Cosmic symbolization in the design of cities found more explicit expression in China than perhaps in any other civilization. The Chinese imperial capital was a diagram of the universe. The palace and the principal north-south axis stood for the Polar star and the celestial meridian. . . . The Four Quadrants in the heavenly vault became the Four Directions or Four Seasons of the terrestrial grid. Each side of the square may be identified with the daily position of the sun or with each of the four seasons.[20] [Yi-Fu Tuan]

Obviously, under such circumstances, it would have been unthinkable to the Chinese to apply the circular aspects of the mandala to the design of their cities.

Practices in India followed the same pattern. Major axes keyed to the four cardinal points of the compass, centrality of palace location, and a rectangular perimeter were the marks of Indian city plans where symbolic objectives were being pursued.[21] Nor did the Burmese depart from similar practices. Ancient beliefs in magical squares as well as religious symbolism again prescribed viewpoints resulting in square and rectangular cities as early as the first century A.D. Although some contact with Chinese planning traditions may account for this, U Kan Hla asserts that Burmese traditions and practices developed independently, even though they led to the same urban consequences:

Many ancient Burmese beliefs are connected with a magical square which symbolized graphically the popular cult of the planets. Burmese astrology recognizes nine planets including the Sun, the Moon, and two fictitious planets, Rahu and Kate. They are closely connected with the cardinal directions, with the days of the week, with sacred animals, and with Buddha's disciples. Each of the nine planets, with its corresponding objects, has a definite position in the magic square (which marvelously resembles the plan of a "square city").[22]

Japan and Korea, lying so much within the shadow of Chinese precedent in so many things, including ritual cities, have also followed it in their planning practices. So have the countries of Southeast Asia with their similar sharing of traditions, influences, and viewpoints.

The absence in the East, therefore, of the circle as prototype symbol for use in the design of an ideal city can be understood in terms of a shared interpretation of the cosmos.* The mandala combines heaven and earth, circle and square; and those things of the earth (such as the city) of necessity must partake of the square to properly employ the sacred and symbolic language. No such inhibitions restrained the West. As a result, all evidence of cities in the round as a planned phenomenon is to be found in those lands lying in or influenced by what is called the Western tradition.

* It is a happy coincidence that the physical properties of the square are well suited to the needs of both agrarian and urban societies, such as the measuring of land, defining of fields and ownerships, and determining of lot sizes and building sites. The circle as a tool for such purposes carries with it heavy liabilities.

II. Circular Cities of the Ancient Near East

IN SPITE of a general agreement that the earliest cities occurred in the Near East, and a recognition of inferences to be made from the form of the Egyptian hieroglyph for "city," the incidence of planned circular cities among ancient Near Eastern urban societies is limited. The symbolism may have been appreciated, but the actual process of building a city was in usual practice left to follow more conventional orthogonal directions. But then that is much of the reason why those that did occur are likely to capture our interest.

Practicality should not be entirely precluded from the rationale of a round plan for a city. If circularity is joined with a radial street plan, citizens have easy and direct access both to the ceremonial core at the center and to the defensive walls at the outer edge. For their length, those walls in turn offer shelter for the largest enclosed area, with considerable saving in effort and cost of construction. And all inhabitants will share, consciously or otherwise, an environment whose geometric purity ties them to a larger view of the universe of which their lives have been made a part. For the ancient world, beset by uncertainties, this could carry with it some reassuring comforts.

On the other hand, where these circularly planned cities were radial as well, there were consequences with considerably less promise for the lives lived in them. Rulers would be able to reinforce their physical and psychic presence and control; the benefits the defenders enjoyed by their speedy access to the walls would be offset by a similar ease of advance by the enemy to the city's center should they break past the walls;

congestion was encouraged by central concentration of institutions and activities; there were problems of street orientation to the sun and prevailing wind patterns; and awkward yard and building site shapes occurred. For some or all of these reasons, a circular city was more likely to enclose an orthogonal street plan than a radial one, both in ancient times and later as well.

But aspects of rationality or irrationality, at least at this stage of the history of these cities, should not obscure the more fundamental inspiration: their role as ritual center. As Paul Wheatley writes, wherever we find primary urban generation,

. . . we arrive not at a settlement that is dominated by commercial relations, a primordial market, or at one that is focused on a citadel, an archetypal fortress, but rather at a ceremonial complex . . . the predominantly religious focus to the schedule of social activities associated with them leaves no room to doubt that we are dealing primarily with centers of ritual and ceremonial. Naturally this does not imply that the ceremonial centers did not exercise secular functions as well, but rather that these were subsumed into an all-pervading religious context.[1]

Given this context, in those instances where the circular city occurred, physical inconveniences would be easily accommodated in the interest of ideological and ritualistic consistency and satisfactions.

Except in its hieroglyphics, Egypt offers no evidence of an interest in circularly-planned cities. But then this poverty of evidence tends to be characteristic of Egyptian urban history in general in a nation whose combination of building materials,

Nile flooding, and attitudes toward things of this earth all combined to weaken the likelihood that ancient urban remains would survive to our own times. Of those that do survive (e.g., Tel-el-Amarna, Kahun), all subscribe to orthogonal techniques.

Instead of Egypt, it was in the region of the Tigris and Euphrates rivers where the earliest and intermittently continuing appearance of planned circular cities occurred. The Sumerians, identified with the beginnings of urban plans laid out with some geometric order, built their settlements with consciousness of the city's unique role as ritual center. The focus was

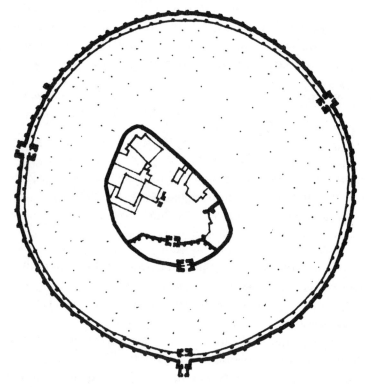

10. *Plan of Zincirli*

on the center, emphasized by its location, its height, and by the architectural treatment of its associated structures, especially the temple ziggurat. This sense of core enhanced the status of the religious, political, and economic functions which emanated from it and of course in material ways gave substance to the vision of the city in its relationship to cosmic laws. A planned circular approach was not far removed from such a vision.

The Hittites, farther north in Antolia, may have come even sooner than the Sumerians to actual planned urban circularity with their city of Zincirli (Zendjirli, Cincirli) founded near the beginning of the first millennium B.C. (fig. 10). This city, however, with its central fortress seems more important as citadel than ritual center, a reflection of the defensive cast of the Hittite mind. The interior planning indicates no formalistic concerns, at least in what has been excavated to date. But how does one explain the near perfection of the circular alignment of its walls, the one hundred regularly-spaced rectangular towers, and the three equally-spaced gates, whose placement suggests concerns for cosmic forms and order that go beyond mere defensive needs?

The Hittites were in due course conquered by the Assyrians (conquerors also of the Sumerians), whose contact with the Hittites and with Zincirli may help explain a bas-relief in the Louvre from Assurbanipal's palace at Nimrud of about 900 B.C. (fig. 11). Its format resembles that of the Egyptian "city" hieroglyph, a circular enclosure with regularly spaced battlements. The four quadrants show various food preparation activities, possibly those of an army camp, though Pierre Lavedan interprets the relief as the representation of a city.[2] Whatever the circumstances, this may well represent a coming together of Tigris-Euphrates urban traditions with those of Anatlia in preparation for what would be more clearly realized cities in the round.

11. Nimrud bas-relief

with an elaborate system of seven concentric walls, each higher than the preceding one. The city's location on a gentle hill enhanced this progression of heights, but Herodotus adds that "it was mainly affected by art." He then describes what would surely have been the most visually dazzling of urban scenes, one which also reinforces the cosmic and sacred implications of planned circular cities. Seven concentric rings of walls gave structure to the city, each painted a different color to identify it with one of the colors assigned to the planets. The outer wall was white (Jupiter), then came black (Mercury), purple (Saturn), blue (Venus), and orange (Mars). The remaining two walls at the center were coated with silver (Moon) and gold (Sun). These latter two also enclosed quarters for the king, the nobility, and the royal treasury. Moving out from the center through the various rings, the assignment of living space reflected a descending order of social rank, much as Chinese imperial cities reflected a similar caste stratification through spatial assignment but in an orthogonal format. The common people of Ecbatana lived beyond the outer walls.[3]

Herodotus' history is more valuable for us in recording the mystique of circular city rituals of his times than as urban history, since neither later visitors to the city nor archaeology has since been able to confirm his description. It must have been too much influenced by contemporary myths. Today's Iranian city of Hamadan, which entirely occupies Ecbatana's site, gives no hint of its ancient predecessor. Ironically, superimposed in recent years over Hamadan's complex fabric as an Islamic city is a sunburst of six symmetrically aligned streets radiating out from a common center and suggestive of ideal city devices mindlessly employed in this case to provide the old city with the trappings of modernity.

Two cities built in the late years of the first millennium B.C. maintain the cosmic city tradition and evoke memories of Zincerli's regularity: Ctesiphon and Darabjerd. Ctesiphon was lo-

Was such a city Ecbatana? Herodotus would have us believe as much, and the detailed account of it in his history does indeed represent what would have been a splendid ritual center in the circular city tradition. Built in 715 B.C. as capital of the Medes after their overthrow of Assyrian rule, the city was located in the plain of today's northwest Iran. Herodotus describes how Deioces, son of Phraortes, a Mede, was made the Medean king to bring order to their fragmented village society. In accepting the crown, he required that a suitable royal city and palace be built. Ecbatana was the result.

According to Herodotus, it was perfectly circular in plan

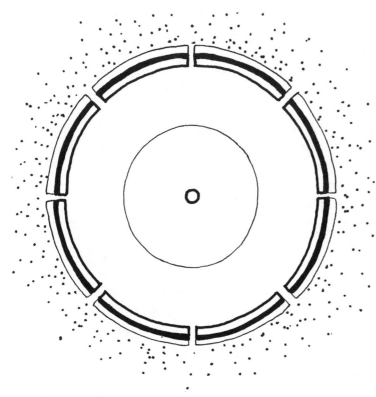

12. Plan of Darabjerd

cated on the Tigris River near modern Baghdad, but little survives except the great brick masonry arch of its former audience hall. Built by the Parthians about 129 B.C. as the winter residence of their kings, the city had walls that were more oval than circular. Darabjerd's plan, however, is a near perfect circle, double walled as at Zincirli with gates and a ditch (fig. 12). Its outer area enclosed an inner enclave defined by a circular wall. Today, traces of roads radiate from this center out to the former wall gates, which are roughly equidistant from each other.[4]

Small wonder, then, that Darabjerd is presumed by Arab

historians to have been the model for the much greater city of Gur (Firuzabad), for there is a basic similarity between the plans of the two cities (fig. 13). Both are located in southern Iran not far from each other: Darabjerd some 165 miles (265 km) east of Shiraz, Gur 75 miles (120 km) south of that same city. Gur was built in 226 A.D. by Ardashir I, the founder of the Sassanian dynasty of Persia and the then recent conqueror of the Parthians. For his new capital he was likely to have been motivated toward ambitious environmental goals; what remains of the city even today suggests Ardashir's ambitions and the extent to which he drew from cosmic city traditions to achieve them.

The city was concentrically and radially planned with a double ring of outer walls, moated between. Enclosed within these perfectly circular walls was a vast inner circle. Four gates oriented to the compass cardinal points admitted roads radiating outward from the center. Other roads led from the center to the outer walls to create a pattern of twelve city sectors named after the signs of the zodiac.[5] Near the center, a third ring wall with four gates defined what is presumed to have been a terraced enclave for officialdom with palace and governmental buildings, the temple, residences for priests, and what was possibly a tower for sacred fires. Today there is scant evidence of what development beyond this civic core might have been. Presumably this was the residential area for the upper and middle classes of the capital; the common folk (as at Ecbatana) lived beyond the walls.

One would not be wrong inferring that Gur embodied the idea of the Parthian/Persian city. The central significance given to the cult of fire makes of the fire tower the true center of the city. The circular configuration of the city corresponds not only with the military camp but also makes the city a representation of the sun disk. . . . Circles and rays symbolize the ascendency of the light and good over dark

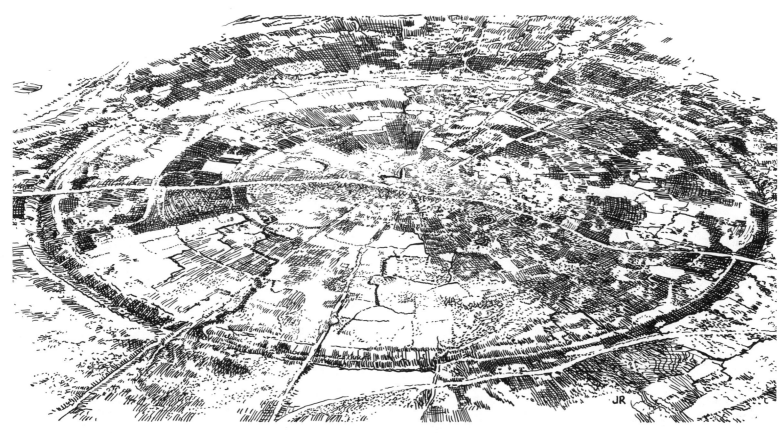

13. *Gur (Rohrer)*

and evil. With this the city becomes a manifestation of cosmic processes.[6] [Ernst Egli]

The Sassanian dynasty, empire, and capital were all destroyed in the seventh century with the coming of Islam and the Arabs. Today, except for the obelisk-like remains of the fire tower, ancient foundations, a small neglected modern mosque, some rather tentative-looking agricultural fields, a lone and venerable juniper tree, and the residue of the ring walls, Gur's site is deserted, barren, and stone-strewn. Still,

the great bowl of the plain on which the city stood and its encompassing distant mountain ring lead one to agree with Ardashir in the location of his capital with its cosmic linkages in plan and form to reflect the power of his dynasty.

Following Islam's spread over the Near East, North Africa, and Spain which began in the seventh century, Arabic practices were to build on those of indigenous peoples contained within the length of the caliphate. Environmental arts throughout the Islamic world reflected this: architecture, gardens, and cities contained linkages with the past but were reinterpreted with new color, richness, and vitality to serve their Arabic sponsors. Above all was Baghdad, the most splendid affirmation of Arabic adaptation of the forms and rituals of the cosmic city.

Like Ecbatana, the modern city of Baghdad retains no hint of its lofty origins. But fortunately we are able to recall the old city through detailed descriptions and measurements which have come down to us from the historians of its day. With ambitions that it should be a "paradise on earth" and the "na-

vel of the universe," Baghdad was to be no anonymous local settlement but a city to capture the imagination of the world of its time, a reputation that lingers even into our own.

The city was founded in 762 as a new capital for the Arabic Abbasid Dynasty in the reign of Caliph al-Mansur. From its beginnings, al-Mansur saw for his city a splendid future. Its official name, Madinat-al-Salam, the City of Peace (or Safety), was chosen for its reference to paradise, drawn from the Koran (Dar-es-Salam). The site on the Tigris River not far from the Euphrates was strategically selected to enhance the city's prospects for political and economic domination of the commercial routes that crossed it and of the region and the Arabic empire beyond.[7] Astronomers determined the propitious moment for the laying of the foundations.

Since Arabic interest and achievement in both astronomy and astrology were considerable, the role of astronomers in the rituals of the new city was appropriate. They must surely have been drawn to the plan of the new city, for al-Mansur had chosen a perfect and cosmic circle (fig. 14). At the time it was claimed that this was the only known example of a circular city. This was, of course, mistaken; Ctesiphon was only a short distance downstream from Baghdad, and both Gur and Darabjerd, though more distant, were a part of the caliphate. The similarities between Baghdad's plan and that of Gur suggest that the inspiration for the new round city had linkages with the capital of that earlier autocratic society. But perhaps it is simply that similar social systems and environmental goals attracted al-Mansur and his planners to the same design precedent as attracted the Sassanians at Gur. More likely, his historians wished to enhance the prestige of their patron by insisting on the uniqueness of his plan for the capital. The effort was redundant; Baghdad's reputation would soon stand on its own.

Contemporary accounts tell of the choice of a circular plan for the enhancement it gave the position and prestige of the

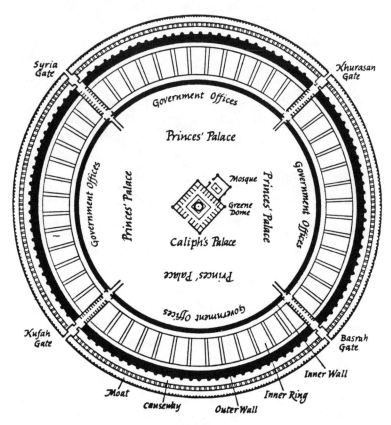

14. *Plan of Baghdad. Reprinted from Philip K. Hitti,* Capital Cities of Arab Islam, *by permission of the University of Minnesota Press.*

monarch located at its center, equidistant to all parts and people of the city. Note also the cosmic implications of the plan in a society oriented to astrology and astronomy and the attraction the form would therefore have. Finally, if we recall Jung and his followers, turning to the circle as a plan choice would simply acknowledge the implications of subconscious engramming. For whatever combination of such motivations, the plan for Baghdad was determined. Jacob Lassner describes its inception:

The overall plan of the Round City seems to have been al-Mansur's personal creation, although the actual task of tracing the city plan was entrusted [to others]. In order to see the form of the city plan, the Caliph ordered that the lines be traced with ashes. . . . When this was accomplished, the Caliph gave the site his personal inspection, walking about and looking at the outline of the *fasils*, gates, arcades, courtyards, and the city moat. He then ordered for cotton seeds which were subsequently placed along the ash marks. The seeds were doused with naphtha and set on fire. After viewing the flaming outline, he commanded that the foundations be laid on exactly these lines. . . .[8]

The city was to be perfectly circular, surrounded by two lines of walls. The outer wall with merlons and towers was of brick, additionally reinforced by a water-filled moat and a great glacis.* The walls were pierced at compass points by four vaulted and gilt-domed gates† opening into wide avenues with brick and plaster arcades which led in radiating patterns to the city's center.

* In fortifications, a long gentle slope beyond the moat clear of all obstacles (see figure 32).
† "The gates had double iron doors that were so heavy they required several men to open and close them. Open, the gates were high enough to allow a horseman carrying a banner or a lance to pass through" (Wiet, *Baghdad*, p. 14).

Baghdad's center, as at Gur, was the walled official precinct. It was a great enclosed courtyard in the middle of which was the Golden Gate Palace of the caliph; its audience hall was topped with a green dome whose 355-foot (108-meter) height made it visible from all parts of the city and the countryside beyond. The principal mosque adjoined the palace. Quarters were also provided in the center for the households of the caliph's younger sons, officers, chief palace officials, the treasury, miscellaneous public offices, and the kitchens.

The arcaded avenues divided the city between the center and the outer walls into four equal quadrants which were residential wards with some 30,000 inhabitants, most likely court employees and the army. Two ring streets, one paralleling the inside line of the outer walls and the other the outer wall line of the palace precinct (but far enough removed to provide an enormous circular esplanade and palace garden around the precinct) served as feeders for the radiating spokes of streets leading off these circumferential rings into the residential quadrants. Employing some 100,000 workmen, within the rather short time of four years the construction of Baghdad was completed. It soon became Islam's most fabulous city. The Arab writer Jahiz wrote of it that he had "visited the greatest cities and those that are the most remarkable in architecture and solidity in the provinces of Syria, in the countries of the Greeks and still others, but I have never seen a city raised to greater heights and more perfectly round, with wider gates, or with such imposing walls."[9]

But the city's plan soon began to lose the purity of its original inspiration, starting the process that led to what we know today, the complete obliteration of the original plan. Baghdad was hardly completed before piecemeal development beyond the walls began to encumber and blur its image. The caliphs themselves contributed to the problem by exiling some urban functions to the city's outskirts. Originally there had been marketplaces for the quadrants, but for security reasons they were removed beyond the walls to suburban and river locations, confining the functions within the walls more and more to the specialized needs of the court. Increasing growth added to the process, the original plan being unable to accommodate all the people attracted to Baghdad, many of whom settled instead in the disorder beyond its walls. Thus by the twelfth century, travelers to the cosmic city of al-Mansur found that his dreams had faded away, the planned city abandoned for a mass of suburban agglomeration. No trace of cosmic Baghdad remains today except that evoked by its literature.[10]

The Near East, generally accepted as the birthplace of the city, also provided the foundations for both the mystique and reality of those planned in the round. Sensitive to cosmic order, people of the ancient Near East built such cities to give substance to that order, for themselves and for others who were to observe them. The transmission of the details of the tradition might be faulty, as with the reporting of Herodotus. But, nevertheless, as the center of events evolved westward into the Mediterranean and Classical world, part of the Near Eastern contribution to those events would include the tradition of the planned circular city.

III. The Classical World's Circular City Theories

THE CLASSICAL WORLD of ancient Greece and Rome did little for the built record of the planned circular city but did much the city's theory which would in due course find flower in later events. The Greeks were not unaware of circular city concepts, but it was through philosophy rather than as builders that they nurtured and transmitted them onward. The Aristotelian universe with its series of concentric shapes surrounding the earth, and the Greek view of humanity as the center of life on earth, indicate a conceptual framework open to further speculative environmental interpretations. The Greeks were also the sponsors of an urban policy of colonization, the most ambitious in the known world of that time. Faced with limited resources for the support of their expanding urban society, they chose wisely to limit gowth in the homeland by developing colonial cities for excess population. Appropriate design and administrative policies for such cities were considered important issues and were therefore the focus of public discussion and speculation.

At its highest theoretical level, the question of urban policy drew Plato into the discourse. Both in the *Laws* and in *Timaeus* he developed his urban model. In the former, the Fifth Book, he required that the city have a central location in its territory with favorable supporting conditions; thereafter the sanctuary for the gods was chosen, the citadel or acropolis, surrounded by a circular wall. Out from this radiated the city, organized like Gur into twelve (zodiacal?) divisions which would also be related to the twelve divisions of the surrounding territory. Population distribution, administration, and support were all linked to this system of territorial division, each of the twelve population groups being assigned a division and a protective god to whom the group or "tribe" was allotted and consecrated.

Special care was to be taken to insure equality in the distribution of resources, territorial and otherwise, among the twelve tribes. Thus, the productivity of each of the city's twelve divisions was equalized by their size, those with rich potential being smaller than those with less promise. Land allotment also was equalized in terms of spatial distance from the city center. Each household would receive two half-sections, one in the city's central area, the other with an outer border location. Population for the city was set at

. . . five thousand and forty individuals—this will give us our brotherhoods, wards, and parishes, as well as our divisions of battle and columns of route, not to mention our currency and measures of capacity, dry and liquid and of weight—to see, I say, how all these details must be legally determined so as to fit in and harmonize with each other.[1]

Plato's *Timaeus* has more cosmological and magical influences, a combination of the ritualized circle and square. Here he is describing Atlantis, an ideal island community. Its plan centered about an inner sacred mount comprised of seven concentric ring walls with a palace (or temple?) at the center. Each of these walls was given a planetary color in a manner similar to that ascribed by Herodotüs to Ecbatana. Surrounding this mount were five encircling zones of land and water. All this central circular complex was located in a great rectangular plain of 60,000 squared plats of ground, a reunion of the two basic geometric elements from the metaphysical mandala tradition of the East.

Plato's search for the ideal city brought him, as it had others, to the formula of the circle. That he chose it in the face of consistently demonstrated and continuing Greek preference for Hippodamian grid-plan regularity reaffirms the inherent attraction of the cosmic and magical properties of the circle. Such isolated architectural examples as the tholoi at both Delphi and Epidaurus indicate the circular plan was not unfamiliar in Greek esthetics. But except for Mantinea's walled outline, Greek use of the circle for planning of cities is unknown. Perhaps Plato's prescription for an ideal city is an amalgam of formalistic themes shaped by his observation of Mantinea in its unique planal setting, Herodotus's illusionary conjectures of Ecbatana with its celebration of Near Eastern and Eastern cosmology, and the psychic presence of inner symbolic attractions, all evidences of Plato's times and of his own oneness with humanity.

Of all the areas dominated by both Greece and Rome, only one city has been included here among those of our specialized group: Mantinea in Greece's Arcadia. K. A. C. Creswell cites it as one of the circular cities known at the time of the founding of Baghdad, and E. A. Gutkind documents his own reasons for granting it that special status. Examining its plan, however, and visiting its site do not clearly tend to reinforce its credentials as one of our select planned cities in the round. Yet it does have some circular characteristics that give it a special place in Greek urban practice.

Mantinea, a city of the fifth century B.C., was destroyed in the fourth century by Sparta. The destruction, however, was not total, and in 371 B.C. its people returned and began the reconstruction process and the building of a new system of walls.[2] Today, these walls are the most convincing evidence of the city's planned circular form. But certainly the famed Greek attention to construction accuracy is not sustained if their goal was a perfect circle: their line is only roughly oval with a series of ten gates opening into the city (fig. 15). The agora and its associated public buildings are located in the approximate center of the walled enclosure with a typical rectangular arrangement that could well be an inheritance from the earlier city. The site suggests also that we are not dealing here with a deliberately-conceived oval plan. Mantinea, unlike so many ancient Greek cities with their irregular sites, was located on a vast plain enclosed by distant hills and mountains. Greek lines of fortifications ordinarily responded to prevailing topographic potentials. Although the city might itself have great regularity in its street plan, its enclosing walls would exploit any defensive advantages that the topography might grant; the resulting wall lines could thus be in sharp contrast to the Hippodamian* order of the streets (e.g., Priene and Miletus on the West coast of Asia Minor). In the case of Mantinea, no such topographic potentials prevailed. The inference therefore seems reasonable that the Greeks in their fortifying of this site built walls on lines drawn expeditiously but not ritualistically equidistant from the agora located at the city center. The outer wall foundations, their length rhythmically broken by regu-

---

* Hippodamus, a somewhat mythical figure of the late fifth century B.C., was identified by Aristotle as having "discovered the method of dividing cities." He was from Miletus, which had been rebuilt in 470 B.C. on a strictly regularized plan, possibly by Hippodamus himself. But to say that he invented such a system overlooks earlier evidence of such practices; his role, rather, was one of clarifying the system through use and example.

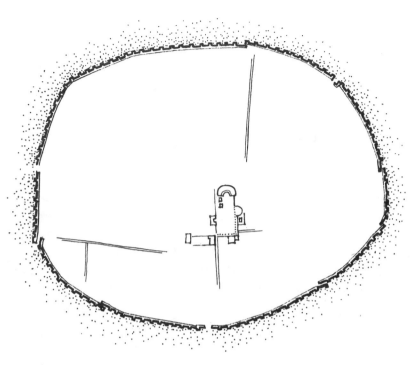

15. *Plan of Mantinea*

larly-spaced rectangular and abutting tower bases, are still to be seen, though portions have disappeared or been broken through for modern roads. Thus, Mantinea, perhaps like Ctesiphon, is more coincidentally than consciously a circular city and is included here because of its uniqueness in Greek urban history rather than because of any direct contribution to the cosmic city tradition.*

* Besides the wall foundations, the best preserved element of Mantinea is the ancient theater. However, a remarkable modern structure has recently been completed in the northwest sector of the ancient city. A church, Haria Photini, seems to combine inspiration from Greece's Mycenaean, Classical, and Byzantine traditions with a strong, even bizarre, personal interpretation by its architect/builder, Konstantinos Paptheodorora. It evokes memories of the work of Antonio Gaudí.

Rome's participation in cosmic city thinking was on an even more theoretical level than Greece's. She did, however, add to the conceptual literature a major source whose impact was to be enormous—but 1,500 years later.

Although no apparent evidence of circular city influence on Roman practice can be found, nevertheless even in Rome's antecedents the roots and legends of circular city thinking emerge. These roots reach back to the Etruscans, whose division of the heavens was a tripartite circular arrangement. Etruscan beliefs had a number of environmental implications, including how the city should be laid out. The north-south east-west *cardo* and *decumanus* axes were especially important.† The heavens and also earth were both considered subject to this fundamental axial discipline. The laying out of a city was overlaid with religious implications for the Etruscans, and they carefully observed appropriate ritual that linked the city with greater cosmic and sacred forces.[3]

The determination of the *cardo* and *decumanus* was an affirmation of the city's identification with the order of the universe. It was also another manifestation of the ways in which people far removed from one another in time and space could return again and again to the same themes. But the practicalities of the matter, including the foundation ritual in which plow and oxen defined the city's outer lines, may have dictated the straight line and the right angle, the *cardo* and *decumanus*, to the neglect of the celestial circle. For the latter is nowhere known to have survived the translation to an urban setting in Etruscan practice (or Rome's either, which was to observe Etruscan precedent). As might be expected, neither of these

† The Etruscan division of the heavens was determined by the cardinal-point orientation of these two intersecting axes. The same divisions were the basis for the laying out of their agricultural fields, sacred precincts, and cities.

peoples was so entranced with theory and ritual in environmental affairs as to neglect pragmatism in real life situations.

The city of Rome was supposedly founded as a circular city; Plutarch describes it as *Roma Quadrata* with a circular perimeter established for it about its center, the *mundus*, by oxen and plow. As explained by Carl Jung,

In each theory [of Rome's founding] a true mandala is involved. . . . It was more than a mere outward form. By its mandala ground plan, the city, with its inhabitants, is exalted above the purely secular realm. This is further emphasized by the fact that the city has a center, the *mundus*, which established the city's relationship to the "other" realm, the abode of the ancestral spirits.[4]

Gutkind, however, discounts this interpretation of Plutarch, noting that "here are clearly two different ceremonies: the digging of the circular pit and the plowing of a furrow, whose course—that is, the shape of the area marked out by the plow—was not an outer circle around the *mundus* but most probably a square or a rectangle."[5] Certainly, accepted Roman practice throughout the history and length and breadth of the empire supported this viewpoint. The *cardo, decumanus*, and rectangular perimeter were to be ubiquitous in Roman colonial cities, which far surpassed Greek achievements in their number and locational spread.

But a curious exception to this Roman orthogonal regularity can be found in the work of the single Roman author whose writings on architecture and city planning have survived to our own time: Marcus Vitruvius Pollio, author of *De architectura libri decem*. Vitruvius was an architect of the age of the emperor Augustus (first century B.C.); he worked in the capital and was familiar with the best contemporary practices. Although the ten volumes of his work deal primarily with architecture and building techniques, the first book contains four

chapters on cities with specific provisions for their siting and planning. He broke with prevailing practice to advance a circular radial plan as the required standard. There is no ambiguity as to his choice; it appeared to carry no trippings of myth or ritual but was entirely based on pragmatism: "Towns should be laid out not as an exact square nor with salient angles, but in circular form, to give a view of the enemy from many points."[6]

Vitruvius, however, was not insensitive to the well-being and convenience of his city's residents, and he chose radial streets and a polygonal outline to serve their needs—but without conscious cosmic linkages. Streets were to be radially organized with orientations based on a Roman misconception as to the transmission of disease, which they ascribed to the winds. An additional refinement had it that winds came from only certain directions: from the four cardinal points and the halfway points between. Since the orientation of streets affected their wind-channeling capacity, it therefore followed for Vitruvius that streets should be organized on a radial pattern in such a way as to exclude the directions from which the winds flowed:

By shutting out the winds from our dwellings, therefore, we shall not only make the place healthful for people who are well, but also in the case of diseases due perhaps to unfavourable situations elsewhere, the patients, who in other healthy places might be cured by a different form of treatment, will here be more quickly cured by the mildness that comes from shutting out of the winds. . . .

Some have held that there are only four winds: Solanus from due east; Auster from the south; Favonius from due west; Septentrio from the north. But more careful investigators tell us that there are eight. . . . Then let the directions of your streets and alleys be laid down on the lines of division between the quarters of two winds.[7]

What resulted was a radial pattern of streets with alignments

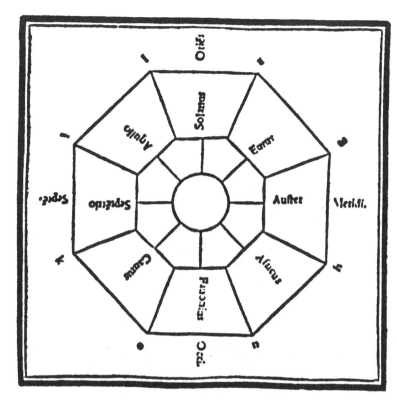

16. *Vitruvian town plan diagram*

His urban vision was preoccupied with the pragmatism of the city's protection. It was circular for defense, polygonal to break the force of the winds, and radial to avoid their direction (fig. 16). No other rationale, ceremonial or otherwise, consciously pertained. One could wish that he might have been moved in his choice by more spacious visions, some hint that by earning benefactions from the gods for the city's cosmic design this would contribute to the social well-being and happiness of the citizenry. But there is no such tempering of the narrowness of his purpose, sanitized thought it was. The Vitruvian message appears, however, to have been at best a minority report for his era. There are no known examples of Roman cities planned on his circular and radial planning principles.

The Classical world's contribution to the planned circular city was theoretical rather than concrete. Nevertheless, it was seminal. Saint Augustine and the disciples who followed in his wake so venerated the *Timaeus* that it assumed an almost biblical stature. A tradition of neo-Platonism was thus built into the foundations of medieval thought and traditions. Vitruvius would assume a similar stature in the theoretical speculations of the Renaissance. Apparently ignored in his own time, this book 1,500 years later was to have an enormous impact on urban theory and, to a lesser extent, on practice. His formalistic rules would then take on an unexpected new vitality, flowing into and becoming an important part of a Renaissance flood of ideal circular city theoretical speculations.

whereby the city perimeter always presented a blank wall to the eight prescribed wind directions.

Although the Vitruvian manuscript contained no diagrams to interpret his design standards, the consequences are clear.

IV. The Circular City of the Medieval World

THE IDEAL CIRCULAR CITY of the medieval world was not of *this* world. There are round medieval cities, but not planned ones; where round cities occur they are most usually the product of spontaneous growth from the center outward with adjustments to the perimeter as circumstances required. Thus we find medieval Nördlingen in Germany with the concentric rings of its streets recording two stages of growth (fig. 17), or Bram in France with a similar evolutionary record in its plan (fig. 18); or—most archaic of all—the Baltic fortress refuge of Eketorp in Sweden, completed 1,500 years ago and believed to be Scandinavia's first urban settlement (fig. 19). All demonstrate how the combination of site, defense, and spontaneous urban growth can result in a remarkable degree of circularity and concentric pattern. The medieval city was not without its symbolisms: the cathedral, the city hall, the guild hall, the marketplace, the castles—all had meanings beyond the immediacy of their specific tasks. But as a circular ensemble the result was unplanned. Ideal cities were not the stuff of daily life but something belonging to a more spiritual and mystic expectation, the kingdom of heaven.

Medieval thought maintained touch with ideal city thinking, however, in its concepts of a Jerusalem both celestial and earthly; when visualization occurred, ancient themes reappeared. Whatever the reality of the city of Jerusalem (and few had visited it), when the medieval artists, illustrators, and map makers sought to picture it in either its earthly or heavenly context, it was in cosmic city terms (fig. 20). As in Augustine's City of God with its perfect circular form, so Jerusalem

17. Plan of Nördlingen

was similarly perceived. Reappearing also was the quadripartite arrangement of crossed streets, the circle and the cross in yet another urban translation.

Saint Augustine (A.D. 354–430) was central to this continuity, for his writings gave expression to ideas that would shape the Middle Ages. For him and those whose thought was built on his precedent, mathematics was the key whose mastery would reveal both earthly and heavenly truth. "Thou hast ordered all things in measure and number and weight" was the Biblical wisdom of Solomon transposed for the purposes of the medieval world's understanding of itself and of the celestial order.[1] To search for perfection was to seek the underlying laws by which it could be explained and reached. For Augustine, these laws were mathematical and modular, revealed both in numbers and in sound, principles that had application most directly to architecture and to music. Contemplation of truths founded on such laws would open the mind to the perception of perfect beauty in which appearances are transcended by di-

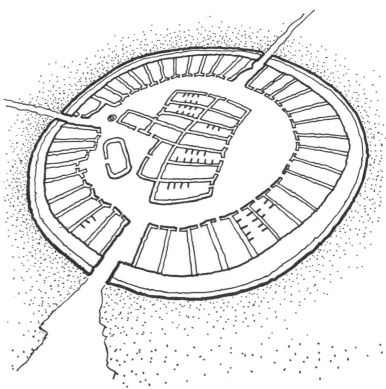

19. *Plan of Eketorp*

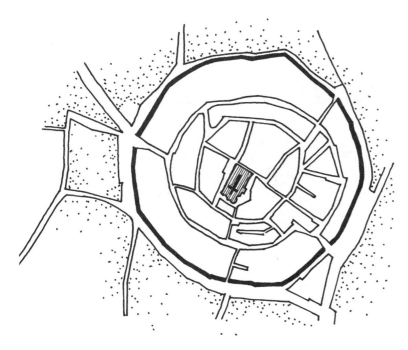

18. *Plan of Bram*

vine revelation. Numerical and musical ratios were reduced by Augustine to a hierarchical ranking. His preference as the most admirable ratio was "that of equality or symmetry, the ratio of 1:1, since here the union or consonance between the two parts is most intimate. Next in rank are the ratios 1:2, 2:3, and 3:4—the intervals of the perfect consonances, octave, fifth, and fourth."[2] All the arts were similarly governed by numerical laws as were also the functions and beauty of the cosmic system and the Celestial City itself.

The cathedral had unique rank in the medieval mind. More than building or even temple, it was the house of God but also an image of heaven, of God's city. The responsibility for its design was therefore awesome, involving the architect in a project whose symbolism drew from the same laws as those underlying heavenly perfection. To contemplate the cathedral was to anticipate the City of God. Such concerns account, therefore, for the degree to which the design of the medieval cathedral—and, by extension, the Celestial City—was founded on the comprehensive application of Augustinian geometry.

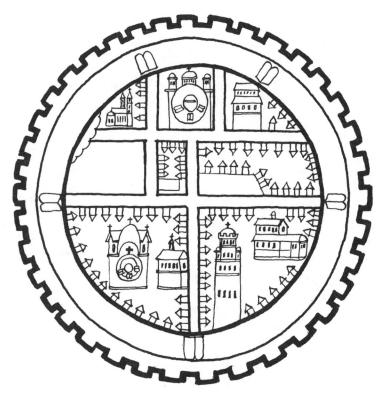

20. *Jerusalem* (*after a twelfth-century* Passionale, *Landesbibliothek, Stuttgart*)

His interpretation of divine order, and the subsequent reinforcement of his own neo-Platonism by his followers and their preoccupation with the *Timaeus*, maintained a tradition of numerical harmony as the basis for achieving beauty and revealing geometrical and divine order. In that order, for Augustine the purest form was the circle.

We are also reminded of medieval familiarity with circular themes by Dante (1265–1321), that "interpreter of all medieval Europe." A monumental figure in Italian letters, Dante was unique in his familiarity with the learning of his day, including Classical and post-Classical authors. In his *Commedia* he is guided by Virgil in his descent through the nine concentric circles of Hell, then ultimately achieves Heavenly Paradise where Beatrice ascends with him to the final ninth "crystalline Heaven" with its choirs of angels who move in nine concentric circles about the figure of God.

Medieval Europe was not without its planned cities, but they were a minor theme in its urban history. Often such cities, or "bastides," would adopt an orthogonal approach, reflecting Roman colonial precedent: they displayed the same rectangular outline of the walls and an internal grid arrangement of streets with intersecting axes meeting at the center, affirming their place in a long line of orthogonal designs for planned colonial settlements. So the linkages of medieval ideal cities with circularity would remain theoretical and inferential, like embers waiting for more favorable conditions, just ahead, before breaking out in active flame.

Considerably outside the geographical context of medieval Europe, but contemporary with it, was the circular city of Mexcaltitán on the west coast of central Mexico. Even though the separation of hemispheres carried with it vast differences in circumstances and outlook, the Mexican city's plan evokes me-

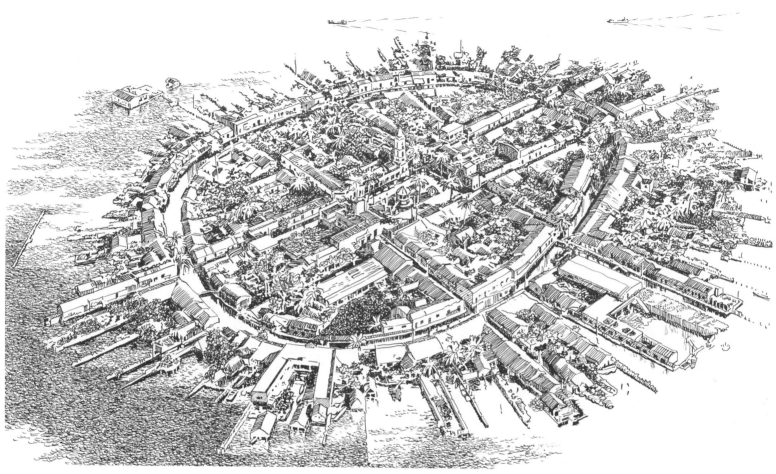

21. Mexcaltitán (Rohrer)

dieval, even Renaissance, values and symbols (fig. 21). Mexcaltitán's origins are lost; Dr. Jiménez-Moreno, a director of the National Institute of Anthropology and History in Mexico City, thinks it reached a high point in the twelfth century, then declined to its present state. It has also been suggested that it was the ancestral home of the Aztecs, whose legends recalled origins on an island in the middle of a lake. There are interesting similarities between the basic planning arrangements of Mexcaltitán and that of the Aztec island capital of Tenochtitlán at the time of the Spanish conquest.[3]

Whatever the circumstances of its past, Mexcaltitán's city plan preserves an ellipse described by an outer street, with internal streets forming a cross. The people there are convinced this is no coincidence but has cosmic significance. They see their city as the center of the universe, the streets forming a cross in the same manner as the heavenly universe is equally quartered (a reappearance of that same theme in the mythology of yet another part of the world). This may explain the extent to which the basic plan has been so well preserved, a singular resistance over centuries to altering its cosmological clarity.[4] It remains a remarkably pure expression of a ritualized approach to the city and its forms and spaces: a circle quartered by streets whose meeting is marked by an open arcaded plaza faced by the church. Both the medieval and Renaissance theorists would have lived comfortably in this ensemble.

The medieval world and especially the Church, its thinkers and its artists, gave a continuity to ancient concepts and practices that would break out with new vitality when more expansive times returned. Thus medieval thought in general and Augustine in particular formed a handsome bridge from the Platonic thought of the Classical age to the ideas that would emerge in the Renaissance. Indeed, the conceptual rationale for the exuberant circular cities of the fifteenth and sixteenth centuries was built on foundations maintained and strengthened by this continuity with the past.

V. Renaissance Circular Cities: Fifteenth and Sixteenth Centuries

WHAT THE PAST had treated as an idealized but accessory theme in its range of urban practices, the Renaissance was gradually to rephrase and give unprecedented attention and stature. In the pantheon of intellectual and artistic enthusiasms and initiatives that was the mark of the Renaissance, the theory of perfect beauty and the striving for its realization had important environmental repercussions. The planned circular city was no longer an arcane conceit; it was now typically included in the theoretical vocabulary of the era. Elements of its conceptual presence were more likely than ever before to have real impact on the cities of its time, whether idealized or secular.

The nature of Renaissance ferment was conducive to such urban stirrings. It was a move toward new concepts, not only of the individual but also of the world and universe. Having worked their way through the medieval spiritual climacteric, human concerns were released by the Renaissance for other appreciations and tasks. From heaven there was a return to earth. The forces of faith, mysticism, and feeling may not have been displaced, but they lost precedence to those seeking logical thought and scientific method. There was an audacity in human objectives which expected through the processes of rationalization and logic to establish laws, rules, and methods for achieving perfection. Philosophers, theoreticians, mathematicians, artists—all were caught up in the intellectual esprit of the Renaissance. Their energies found expression in a variety of ways, including the pursuit of new spatial concepts and goals.

The Ptolemaic metaphysical concept of the universe was to give way to the Copernican revolution with its rational and systematized cosmology. The world was released from immobility to become a participant in a perfect universal order of perpetually circling bodies. There was a supportive harmony between Renaissance arts and this new scientific understanding of the universe; both were discovering means to explain and express spatial order in which all parts shared in an interrelated scheme that reflected an underlying logic.

The individual was also given a new priority in the Renaissance scale of values with its focus on human characteristics and concerns. The body itself was to become the subject of investigation both for an appreciation of its beauty and for an understanding of its being. The individual was seen in terms emphasizing potentials for versatility and creativity; avenues of investigation which had been largely closed off in the medieval past were again made accessible. Human experiences and achievements, both present and past, were studied for understanding and inspiration. This was especially so for the learning of Classical antiquity, which assumed special status as a kind of foundation for the structure of Renaissance humanism and its glorification.

This humanism, the focus on the individual, had a unique

translation in physical terms in the emergence of mechanical perspective during the fifteenth century. The medieval arts had essentially ignored perspective in the treatment of space, both in painting and in the city. But with the new perspective technology, the Renaissance had a device for accurately expressing three-dimensional space on a flat surface; it did so in terms of what the individual would see from a single point of view (fig. 22). This was an almost literal transposition of philosophical humanism into artistic terminology and gave expression to an enthusiasm that was immensely influential in reshaping the visual arts, including that of the city.

Out of such circumstances, it is not surprising that the Renaissance mind would be attracted to the ideal city. Renaissance cosmological concepts, humanism, mathematics, technologies, and the arts were supportive of its geometrical patterns and theoretical abstractions and contributed generously to its record. The straight street, the radiating or grid-plan order, the focus of central place, the symmetry of circular and polygonal walls, and star-shaped bastions—all were likely to tantalize minds boldly committed to the search for an ideal city. Urban theorists employed these themes with an unprecedented expansion of the literature, and contemporary painters and architects were to add significantly to the stock of such ideal city visualizations. In turning to the planned circular city as ideal city formula, the Renaissance reaffirmed the pull of an attraction that has already been seen as venerable.

For a body of thought whose theoretical nature tended to encourage written expression, the coincidence of the Renaissance and the printed book was a happy one. As a result, in contrast to previous periods, the contemporary literature of ideal city speculations looms large. Participants were varied: architects especially, but also philosophers, engineers, humanists, and other theorists. For all their diversity, however, they had a common loyalty to the circle as inspiration for their idealizations. In the words of Rudolf Wittkower, "the geometry of the circle had an almost magical power over these men."[1]

The Renaissance was a time when many individuals were given to contemplating the nature of utopia and its urban manifestations in the ideal city. The Renaissance personality was attracted to challenging the world and had the temerity to think that what could be changed could be perfected. In times of considerable intellectual and social flux, a search for utopia is a characteristic response: to find solutions for individual happiness, and to offer physical environments whose design is calculated to contribute to it. Thus, the city was viewed as an integrated work of art expressive of levels of beauty and perfection to match the designer's aspirations for the quality of life it was to contain. The irony was that the newly-discovered appreciation for the individual was sacrificed to the dictates of communal codes, behaviors, and laws reinforced by the absolutes and symmetries of utopian and ideal city forms.

These utopias were progressive in as much as they wished to abolish . . . the old economic slavery by a new one: men ceased to be the slaves of their masters or employers, to become the slaves of the Nation and the State. . . . the individual is obliged to follow a code of laws or of moral behavior artificially created for him.[2] [Marie Louise Berneri]

The absolutism of the forms of the Renaissance ideal city anticipated the social and political autocracies of the Baroque prince, who would borrow generously from those forms for his own autocratic purposes.

As participants in the Renaissance enthusiasms of their times, utopians in their search for ideal form were able to draw from Classical guidance and to invoke its authority. Both Plato and Vitruvius served these purposes, at least to the extent of providing appropriate ancient credentials for ideas on which

22. *Renaissance perspective* (*Serlio,* Architettura et prospectiva, *1619*)

the Renaissance then expanded. Neo-Platonism and visualizations of the Celestial City handed on by medieval scholars provided Renaissance utopians with literal and respected precedent to launch their own interpretations of circular form. As for Vitruvius, though he was well known in medieval monasteries, his "rediscovery" in the fifteenth century and the many publications of his book that followed both in Italy and elsewhere in Western Europe made for timely additions to the library of Classical resources to which the thinkers of the day turned. Neither Plato nor Vitruvius offered visual models, but their generalized affirmation of circular and radial approaches provided generations of utopians with sufficient foundations to expand and modify for contemporary purposes, whether in fifteenth- and sixteenth-century Italy or, as their ideas circulated into northern Europe, among theoreticians there as well, especially in France and Germany.

This application of the circular model for urban purposes was further influenced by Vitruvius in a less direct way. The Renaissance search for perfection was attracted to his examination of the architectural problem of designing temples. Such projects called for the highest standards of design goals, for forms most expressive of ideal beauty. His Third Book emphasized symmetry and proportion for these purposes and analyzed the human body as a reflection of a system of perfection and harmony achieved by nature. He offered a human figure which, when its arms and legs were extended, was shown to fit exactly into a circle and square (fig. 23). For the Renaissance theorist here was further proof of the validity of the geometry of ideal forms.

With the Renaissance revival of the Greek mathematical interpretation of God and the world, and invigorated by the Christian belief that Man as the image of God embodied the harmonies of the Universe, the Vitruvian figure inscribed in a square and a circle became

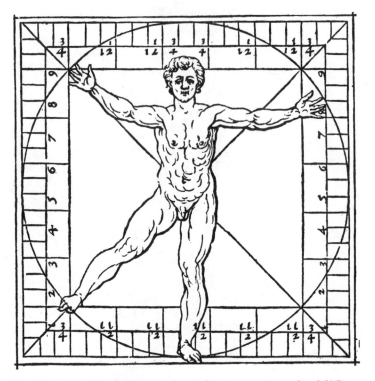

23. *Vitruvian figure (Scamozzi, Architettura universale, 1615)*

a symbol of the mathematical sympathy between microcosm and macrocosm. How could the relation of Man to God be better expressed, we feel now justified in asking, than by building the house of God in accordance with the fundamental geometry of square and circle?[3] [Rudolf Wittkower]

Thus the search for perfect order, for proportional harmonies derived from fundamental relationships reduced to numerical laws and ratios in the Augustinian tradition, found continuity in the Renaissance. Temples designed in observance of these laws with plan forms selected from a geometric hierarchy and interpreted in the architectural vocabulary of Classicism were linked to the medieval cathedral by their shared underlying rationale. A centrally-planned building crowned by the majesty of drum and cupola was the culmination in the Renaissance of the long search for an architecture attuned to divine harmonics (figs. 24, 25). Bramante's Tempietto at San Pietro in Montorio (Rome, 1502–10); Santa Maria della Consolazione by Cola di Matteuccio di Caprarola (Todi, 1508–12); and, most especially, Bramante's central plan for the new Saint Peter's, followed by Michelangelo's dome,

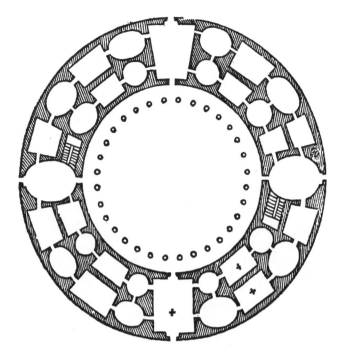

25. *Cataneo, circular church plan*

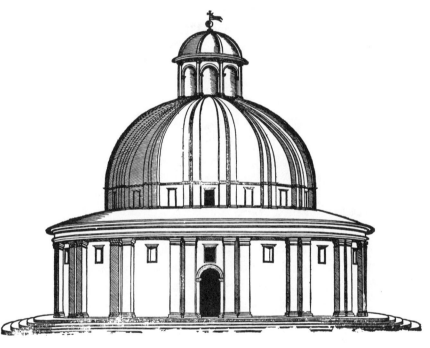

24. *Centrally-planned circular church*
(*Cataneo*, I quattro primi libri, *1554*)

Christendom's supreme temple (begun 1506): all are distillations of centuries of search for perfect beauty. And if rules for ideal form were applicable for the perfect temple, obviously they could be extended to the building of an ideal city.

A design foundation for such a city was provided, based on geometric forms with universal and eternal properties associated at the highest level with beauty, truth, and godliness. The result was the planning of a series of crystalline concentric cities of circular and polygonal variations. They were carefully organized with permutations and perspectives of radials, grids, and open spaces. Within a city's fixed symmetrical constellation of solids and voids, various public and private structures of uniform heights and continuous facades were assigned ordained positions. From the fifteenth through the eighteenth century, the Western world was to be hypnotized by the forms, if not necessarily the spirit, of the ideal city.

The Renaissance Ideal City Theorists

The Renaissance search for ideal form for cities was begun by the Florentine Leone Battista Alberti (1404–72) with his *De re aedificatoria*, first published in Latin in 1485. An architect who combined a great versatility of talents, he carried forward the investigation which would be picked up and further developed by others, both in his own country and beyond. He joined Vitruvius and Augustine in the prescription of the circle as the most desirable geometric shape for the designer to choose, though noting a hierarchy of other choices:

It is manifest that Nature delights principally in round Figures, since we find that most Things which are generated, made or directed by Nature, are round. . . . We find too that Nature is sometimes delighted with Figures of six Sides; for Bees, Hornets, and all other kinds of Wasps have learnt no other Figure for building their Cells in their Hives, but the Hexagon. . . . The Polygons used by the Ancients were either of six, eight, or sometimes ten sides. The Angles of such Platforms should all terminate within a Circle, and indeed from a Circle is the best Way of deducing them; . . .[4]

Although he saw the circle as most directly applicable to churches, Alberti also recognized its desirability in the planning of cities; it offered the kind of geometric equilibrium meant to convey a sense of harmonious integration of all parts, and was thus equally suitable for the centrally-planned church and for its surrounding ideal city. In his Eighth Book he ac-

knowledges that the city's site will recommend different design approaches (e.g., a hill is not so likely to accommodate the versatility of plan selection as a location on an open plain). But nevertheless, "we may conclude that of all Cities, the most Capacious is the round One."[5] In his round city he preferred a street "straight and broad, which carries an Air of Greatness and Majesty," but even here he permitted irregularity if in small towns more defense was thereby provided. Criteria were also established for the locations and uses of public squares within the city and for the quality of public buildings:

. . . their being all laid out and contrived beautifully and conveniently, according to their several uses; for without Order, there can be nothing Handsome, Convenient or Pleasing. . . . It will add much to the Beauty of the City, if the Shops for particular Trades stand in particular Streets and Districts in the most convenient Parts of the Town . . . ; but all nasty, stinking Occupations should be removed out of the Way, . . .[6]

Amenities such as paving, porticoes for shade, controlled building height, arched street entrances, and gardens added to the comfort and beauty of Alberti's ideal city. Fortifications were also mentioned, but only in passing; they were not yet the preoccupation they would later become.

Like Vitruvius, Alberti had no illustrations accompanying his text, so the exact visual recommendations for his city in the round remained inferential. But Antonio Averulino (called Filarete; c. 1400–69) filled that gap with his *Il trattato d'architettura*, first published between 1451 and 1465. An architect and sculptor, Filarete produced the first diagrammatic description of a Renaissance ideal city (fig. 26). Extending Alberti's thinking (on which *Il trattato* was primarily based), his fellow Florentine provided continuity with Platonic and Vitruvian ideals. Filarete's city was presented in plan as an eight-pointed

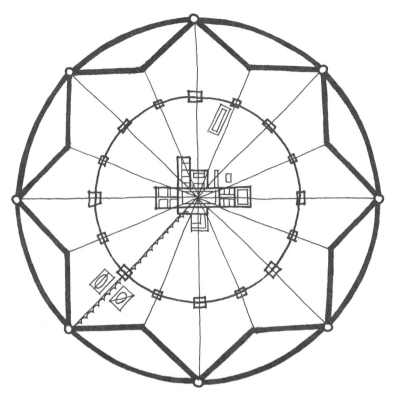

26. *Filarete, plan of Sforzinda*

star contained within a circular wall approached via eight
streets radiating from the central square and its public buildings. Named Sforzinda after his tyrant patron, Francesco
Sforza of Milan, the city's diagram was accompanied by Filarete's description: "The basic form is two squares, one atop the
other without the angles touching. One angle will be equidistant from two other angles in each square."[7] How he proposed
to meld the orthogonals of the civic center and the pattern of
most of the city streets with the city's radials, Filarete did not
say.

The eight-pointed outline of the city moved beyond Alberti
in its recognition of defensive needs. The nature of warfare
was undergoing change, and whereas Alberti's walls followed
essentially medieval precedent, Filarete hinted at improved
military facility, a theme which in the future would become
an end in itself. His system of decentralized neighborhood plazas also showed his acuteness, suggesting he had learned from
the amenities offered by the presence of small neighborhood
open spaces in Italian medieval towns and rightly judged the
ways such plazas could contribute to the life style of his new
one. Bringing water into his ideal city was another means for
adding to its pleasures and safety. Thus Filarete, who did not
have Alberti's aristocratic origins, based his city's plan on a formula for beauty but also equipped it with homelier virtues calculated to add quality to the lives of its inhabitants. Its combination of "commoditas" and "venustas" was offered not for the
glorification of God but for the enhancement of human life.
Beauty was the integrating medium by which all parts found
their place within a work of art—an early "City Beautiful."
That this totality with its debts to Alberti would be neglected
by later followers should not obscure the extent of Filarete's
practical humanism and the contribution he and Alberti made
to the Renaissance tradition. Indeed, the format of their message, if not its more generous qualities, had been reinforced
for the future: the circle was to become an *idée fixe* for most
utopians.[8]

Filarete was followed some twenty years later by another
ideal city theorist in the person of the Sienese Francesco di
Giorgio Martini (1439–1502). An architect, sculptor, and
painter, Martini built on the foundations established by Alberti
and Filarete but added considerable detail and versatility to
them. Martini's plans emphasized the central square and the
city's perimeter with a number of polygonal wall alternatives
(fig. 27). Comparing the city square to the navel of the human
body, he offered it in various forms—polygonal, circular, and

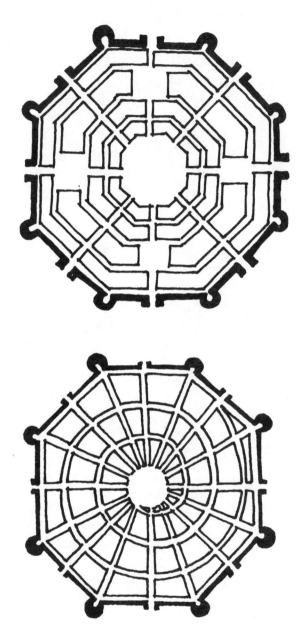

27. *Martini, ideal cities*

rectangular—coordinating the square with the outline and pattern of the city's plan. The walls were also varied in their treatment, going beyond Filarete in their recognition of the city's defensive needs and the ways wall design could contribute to those requirements. The intervening city space between the square and walls was presented in a number of ways. The radial plan, of course, followed the lead of his precedessors, but Martini offered other choices as well. Thus, the grid plan could be recommended for level sites; for hill sites one proposal even featured a combination of radial and spiral patterns. His tendency, however, continued to be a reliance on radial schemes. They were, after all, a more efficient means for connecting the defensive resources at the center to the city's protective walls, no matter what the direction of attack. Martini, whether consciously or not, thus became one of the first to begin moving the ideal city thinking of the Renaissance away from its more theoretical ambitions and toward more explicit military applications.[9]

So far, ideal city plans had been presented entirely as two-dimensional concepts. Their three-dimensional realizations were either left unstated or to be drawn by inference from the accompanying text. A drawing attributed to Fra Giovanni Giocondo (c. 1435–1515), however, gives more body to the Renaissance vision (fig. 28).* A number of confirmations appear in it: the round centrally-planned and domed monumental building at the city's center, radial street plan, uniform building forms, a monumental entrance gate, and the essentially medieval character of the circular surrounding walls. It could easily have been the illustration Alberti failed to give his readers. At this date (c. 1500), the ideal city appears still to have expressed an essentially civilian and peaceful optimism.

* E. A. Gutkind notes that there is no definite proof for this attribution; it was copied by du Cerceau from the original in the sixteenth century (*Urban Development in Southern Europe*, p. 123).

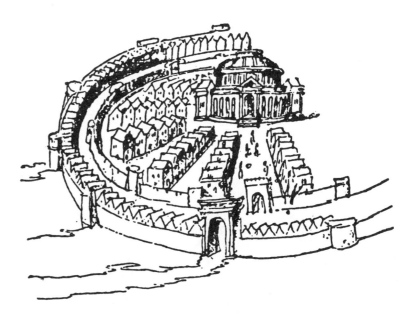

28. *Giocondo, ideal city*

The trend in the sixteenth century began to accelerate toward what Martini anticipated: increasing preoccupation with the ideal city as a fortress rather than an enclave of peaceful pursuits. Pietro di Giacomo Cataneo (?–1569) substantiated this with a series of planned polygonal towns whose fortified rings clearly reflected an exploitation of the walls for their defensive potential (fig. 29). For the first time we see the curtain walls and triangular bastions which would soon dominate Renaissance and Baroque cities, planned or otherwise, their art eclipsed by engineering. Cataneo had worked for an architect who had been influenced by Martini (Baldassare Perruzzi, who had himself attempted some ideal city plans), so Cataneo was no doubt familiar with Martini's line of thought. Cataneo's *I quattro primi libri di architettura* (publication began in 1554) proved to be a kind of pattern book for square and polygonal cities enclosing mostly variations of grid plans. Through the

29. *Cataneo, ideal cities*

succeeding two centuries of preoccupation with the technology of fortification, Cataneo continued to be a source of reference.

Filarete's influence reached forward 150 years to the work of the architect Vincenzo Scamozzi (1552–1616), who acknowledges as much in his *L'idea della architettura universale* (published in 1615 and reissued in many later editions). This dependence on past precedent was characteristic of Scamozzi's work; his main contribution was to synthesize what had gone before in his chapter on the planning of ideal cities (fig. 30). The Cataneo-like grid pattern for his city incorporated one central and four neighborhood squares as well as a rather

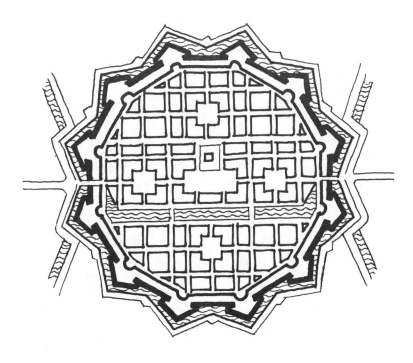

30. *Scamozzi, ideal city*

splendid cross-city internal canal, clearly following in Filarete's path though with much greater explicitness and coordination. All was surrounded by dodecagonal walls with bastions and ditches. Scamozzi's interests specifically extended to fortifications; his *Architettura* included chapters and plates on their design and technology. Yet Scamozzi maintained that "artistic consideration should supersede even the technical needs of fortifications," a lingering loyalty to earlier Renaissance idealism.[10]

That idealism can also be found in the work of Tommaso Campanella (1568–1639), a poet, philosopher, and enthusiast of Galileo and the new astronomy. His speculations (published in 1623 as *Città del sole,* or *City of the Sun*) emphasized an ideal scheme of society which his city would be designed to house. But even coming from that direction, when confronted with the need for creating a design for his city, Campanella could not free his imagination from entrenched cosmic precedent. His circular city on a hill made no significant break with the past in its configurations and, indeed, even recalled memories as far back as Herodotus' account of Ecbatana and Plato's *Timaeus.* Campanella describes it in a "poetical dialogue between a Grandmaster of the Knights Hospitallers and a Genoese Sea-Captain, his guest," as

. . . divided into seven rings or huge circles named from the seven planets, and the way from one to the other of these is by four streets and through four gates, that look toward the four points of the compass. Furthermore, it is so built that if the first circle were stormed, it would of necessity entail a double amount of energy to storm the second; still more to storm the third; and in each succeeding case the strength and energy would have to be doubled; so that he who wishes to capture that city must, as it were, storm seven times. For my own part, however, I think that not even the first wall could be occupied, so thick are the earthworks and so well fortified is it with breastworks, towers, guns, and ditches.[11]

Obviously, even the seventeenth-century utopian mind was never far removed from military realities.

Each successive wall of Campanella's city, decorated with paintings representing all the sciences (mathematics, geography, botany, zoology, etc.), featured galleried palaces that followed the inside circumference of the wall and faced an adjoining ring of open space. These successive rings of walls, palaces, and open space centered about an inner circular space in which was located a round and domed church "built with wonderous art."

This combination of astrology and Christianity could not fail to lead to the adoption of the Copernican picture of the world in which men like Campanella believed. His plan for the City of the Sun was the reflection of this system on earth: the seven concentric rings surrounding the sun were repeated in his design. There can hardly be any doubt that Campanella was strongly influenced by the heliocentric system of Copernicus. The name of his city points directly to this source.[12] [E. A. Gutkind]

Campanella had a lifelong enthusiasm for prophecy and astrology which no doubt had an impact on this thinking. As did other aspects of the Renaissance, his ideas reflected the contrasting influences of rationalism and superstition. The former was never able to release him from the latter nor from the cosmic city's rigidities and rituals.

The route of Renaissance change moved northward from Italy into France and Germany where circular ideal city inspiration began to appear in the sixteenth century. The attraction the French Renaissance architect Jacques-Androuet du Cerceau the Elder (c. 1500–84) felt for it has already been noted in his copying of Giocondo's sketch, but his *Livre d'architectura* (1559) confines itself to circular and symmetrical plans for buildings, Italian inspired.

In a German architect/theorist we have a more clearcut circular city enthusiast: Daniel Speckle (or Speklin, 1536–89) presents in his *Architectura von Vestungen* (1589) both an ideal plan and an indication of ways it could benefit the society it was to shelter (fig. 31). As his title implies, the city's polygonal plan has a domineering line of fortifications. Much about the plan suggests a prototype by Martini; the difference is in the extent to which the fortifications have taken on an increasing dimension of extravagance: walls and bastions now supplemented by star-shaped scarps, counterscarps, ditches, and glacis (fig. 32).

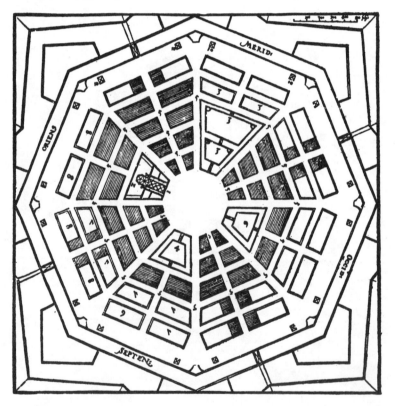

31. *Speckle, ideal city*

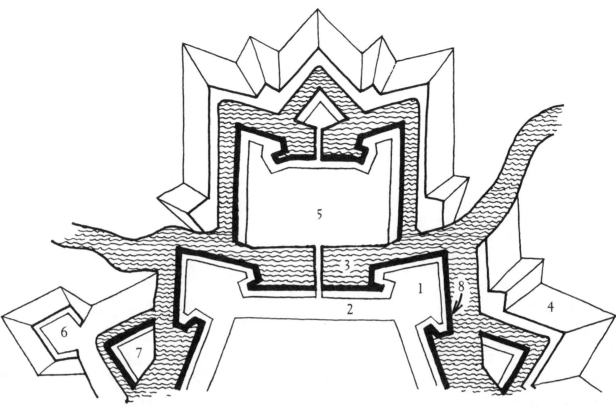

32. *Fortifications glossary*
   1. *Bastion*   5. *Hornwork*
   2. *Curtain wall* 6. *Lunette*
   3. *Ditch*   7. *Ravelin*
   4. *Glacis*   8. *Scarp*

The description of Speckle's city, however, shows an interesting combination of design and social concerns. The church's central location and presence served to uphold proper moral and social standards, reinforced by the nearby ducal palace and town hall; paved streets, primarily for residential use, were lined by well-built stone houses of uniform appearance; locations were established for convenient markets; stables and hospital were to be located so that prevailing breezes would remove their fumes from the city; and storage facilities for grain, fruit, meat, and fish were to have locations that would benefit from those breezes. The city architect was housed in one of the outer areas of the city to be more accessible for the supervision of repairs and maintenance of the walls. The treasury would be supported by an income tax paid by residents for the city's maintenance and public purchases. Limits were even placed on the authority of the local lord in the interests of the common good. In all, Speckle visualized a mechanically well-ordered city that would contribute to a similar order in the society it had been designed to house.

In spite of Speckle's example, the trend was toward viewing the city as fortress rather than as symbol, philosophy, and ideal. The vision of the utopians was being succeeded by that of men whose concern was entirely pragmatic: exploitation of ideal forms for their fortification potentials. They too published, providing both text and diagrams to reveal the ways in which the star-shaped circular city and the nature of Renaissance military technology, especially cannon fire, were bound to be symbiotic. But it was mostly a technical route they chose to follow, with no gesture toward an interest in three-dimensional qualities, spatial imagination, or enhancement of human life. They were captured by the ornament of the ideal city but contributed little to its development as an idea beyond its defensive potential.

The latter part of the sixteenth century would see an increasing production of these publications, which drew heavily on the work of earlier theorists. As their main point of departure, they took the thinking of Cataneo and Scamozzi, plans expropriated for endless mechanical play with forms and outlines of walls, bastions, and earthworks to create extravagantly expensive lines of defense (fig. 33).*

The goals of the military engineer were not antithetical to those of the urban theorist. Both preferred broad straight streets, one because of their military efficiency, the other for their monumentality. Radial and grid plans were more or less equally attractive and can be found in the literature of both designer groups.

Military architects eagerly adopted the radial city plan when they realized that it greatly enhanced the potential strength of their ideal enceintes by providing them with an extremely efficient system of interior communications. . . . In short, the advantages of the radial street plan to the new system of fortification were so obvious that most theoretical treatises did not even feel it necessary to comment

33. *Marchi, fortress*

---

* Pierre Lavedan notes typical titles, including *Della architettura militare* (Francesco de Marchi, c. 1540); *Della fortificazione delle città* (Girolamo Maggi, 1564); *Della architettura militare* (Antonio Lupincini, 1582); *Nuova invenzione de fabbricare fortrezze di varie forme* (Giovanni Bellucci, 1598); *Fortifications et artifices* (Jacques Perret, 1601); *Traité de la fortification* (J. Errand de Bar-le-Duc, 1600); and *L'Architecture militaire* (Adam Fritach, 1635). See Lavedan, *Histoire de l'urbanisme: Renaissance et temps modernes*, p. 17.

upon them. And the plan's almost universal acceptance among military architects is attested by Antonio Lupicini, whose only reference to the street plan of the ideal city in his treatise is the dry comment that it has been laid out "as it is done in modern fortification."[13] [Horst de la Croix]

The future lay with the military planners; the urgency of defense not only caught up the engineers but came to be an increasingly important theme with the humanists, architects, and artists as well. The sketchbooks of Leonardo da Vinci and the career of Michelangelo attest to the scope of defensive preoccupations. In an era of emerging and aggressive national states, border defenses called for the founding of new cities as centers of military strength. Contemporary needs and the characteristics of the planned circular city were thus joined. The latter's form, removed from its theoretical origins, was now exploited for purely practical reasons, and this would continue through the seventeenth and eighteenth centuries. In such an atmosphere, the traditional identification of circular cities with cosmic and symbolic ideas was to be dissipated in a melange of trigonometry, cannon fire traceries, and bombardment analyses. Though they might on occasion revert back to nobler origins, cities in the round would on the whole never regain the expansive and philosophical aspirations with which they once went hand in hand.

Renaissance Circular City Applications

While the fifteenth and sixteenth centuries saw an outpouring of bibliographic enthusiasm for the planned circular city, praising both its theoretical and military attractions, the number of such cities actually built was limited. The Renaissance might have been a time for conceptual speculations, for free-floating philosophical and technical ruminations, but their translation into the stone, tile, and timber of a new city required communal resources not easily marshaled to such an ambitious and costly task. Lewis Mumford notes the slow recovery that Europe had made following the ravages of the Black Death of the fourteenth century when a third to a half of the population was lost. Though by the 1500s there had been a physical recovery, it was still insufficient to restore the vitality of community life and effort of the years preceding that dark century.[14] Renaissance society and its prince were still participants in recuperative social and political processes that led directly to the centralized state and unlimited authority and resources of the Baroque monarch, who was splendidly equipped to indulge in the drama of the city as a coordinated and extravagant work of art. In the meantime, the Renaissance prince was more likely to content himself with adjustments or extensions to his medieval cities, goals more realistically scaled to the energies of his times and the contents of his purse. Circular and centrally-planned environments, when realized by the Renaissance, were usually the work of a painter or an architect of an individual building, art forms for which the necessary resources were more easily available.

Under such circumstances, Italy, the source of Renaissance initiative, would not be the place where the earliest of the planned circular cities were built. Italian authority was too harassed and fragmented, her ambitions and resources too local, to be put to such a task, appreciated though it might have been. Instead, one of the Renaissance's earliest unified national states, one with both political and economic backing for making bold gestures, would be the sponsor: the Spain of Charles V. King and emperor, Charles had an authority that spread over Hapsburg holdings in Central Europe; the Netherlands, Luxembourg, and Franche-Comté; the kingdoms of Naples, Sicily, and Sardinia; Spain and Spanish America. His lands jeopardized by rebellious subjects and nationalistic neighbors, Charles was less likely to be drawn to the circular city's cosmic implications than to its stronghold potentials. The Netherlands represented such an area under stress. In an effort to secure its borders with France, Charles ordered the creation of two fortified towns not far from each other in what is today Belgium: Marienbourg and Philippeville.

These two towns are both transitional rather than fully realized examples of Renaissance planned circular cities. Marienbourg, the first of the two, was begun in 1542 at a time when the Netherlands had for its governor the emperor's sister, Mary

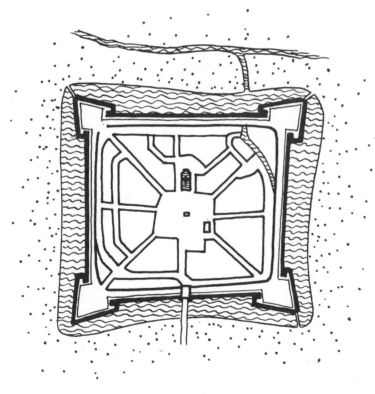

34. *Plan of Marienbourg, 1649*

of Hungary. The town was Vitruvian in its radial plan, all eight streets leading from a spacious central square out to the town's perimeter (fig. 34). The fortifications (whose development continued through the century) were, however, more reminiscent of medieval bastides than of the Renaissance; they formed a square with four triangular bastioned corners. A ditch separated the town from the surrounding countryside. The streets were lined uniformly with the continuous facades of the houses, the interiors of the triangular blocks left open for gardens. An inside perimeter road paralleled the surrounding walls, adding to their adjacent open space and permitting the easy movement of men and equipment for their defense. The designer of this little fortress town is unknown, though the name of Jacques du Broeck de Mons has been associated with it and with the emperor's engineers.[15] It was conquered by the French, who in due course had the walls destroyed. Today Marienbourg is a small and compact country town with some sprawl outward from the former line of the walls that is obscuring its earlier crisp definition.

Philippeville, founded by Charles on 1 October 1555 and named for his father, Philip I, was the work of Sebastian van Noyen, a Dutch architect.[16] The town shared Marienbourg's radial street plan and rectangular town square, though in this case there was an additional circumferential street halfway between town square and walls, and the outline of those fortified triangular-bastioned walls was a pentagon. Some advance is suggested here: abandonment of Marienbourg's right-angled walls, increasingly inefficient under cannon fire, for the improved resistance of walls with more deflective versatility as well as improved lines of fire for their defenders. There comes through, too, a closer approximation of ideal city form, though no doubt in response to its pragmatic conveniences. Later years were to add considerably to the fortified complexity of the town, with bastions, scarps, and glacis (fig. 35). But all

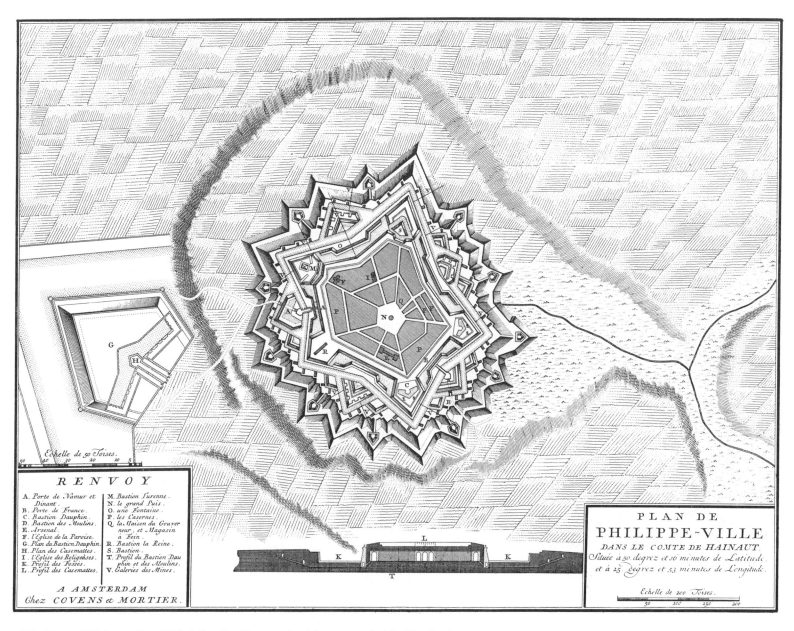

Echelle de 50 Toises.
50   40   30   20   10   5

PLAN DE
PHILIPPE-VILLE
DANS LE COMTE DE HAINAUT.
Située à 50. degrez et 16 minutes de Latitude.
et à 25. degrez et 53 minutes de Longitude.

Echelle de 200 Toises.
50   100   150   200

35. Plan of Philippeville, 1710 (after fortifications had been extended by Vauban)

these are now gone; only hints of their former presence, as Philippeville has grown into a small city in modern times. The old inner street pattern, the town square, and a few buildings of modest historical interest are the only reminders of its distinctive urban origins.

Close connections between Italy and the Hungarian royal court of the sixteenth century account for the appearance of ideal cities in Central Europe. King Matthias Hunyady-Corvinus had ordered a Latin translation of Filarete, a reflection of his interest in and patronage of architecture; his enthusiasm served as a stimulus for the spread of Renaissance ideas into Central Europe just as the French court played a similar role in Europe's west. Slovakia, a part of the Hungary of those days and an area of considerable resources, was to be an early participant in the new enthusiasm with the construction of Nové Zámky (fig. 36).

Begun in 1573 by order of the Emperor Maximilian on a plan by O. Baldigara, Nové Zámky was to anticipate the French Neuf Brisach, with which its plan had much similarity, by over a hundred years. Its hexagonal walls, with typical triangular bastions and ditch, enclosed a similarly-shaped grid of orthogonal streets arranged about a rectangular town square, one corner of which was occupied by the church. The two gates opening into the city were situated exactly opposite each other for total axial symmetry.

Nové Zámky was part of the country's defense system against the Turks, who were a continuing threat to Central Europe at that time, and it later became a strong point among European fortifications. It ceased being a fortress after the destruction of its walls in 1724, continuing as an urban center in present-day Czechoslovakia.[17] But in its day it was a rather remarkable application of ideal city concepts of the Renaissance theorists in an area considerably removed from the centers of their contemplation.

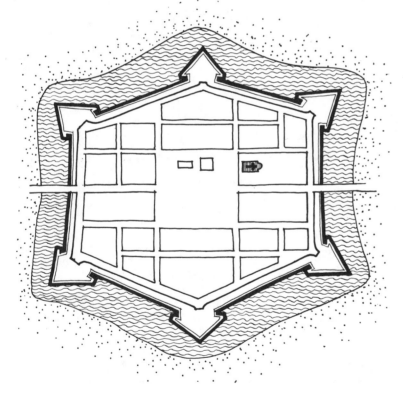

36. *Plan of Nové Zámky, 1595*

Given the rather extravagant gesture which the planned circular city tends to represent, its record in Dutch practice is more substantial than might be expected. The Netherlands of the late sixteenth century comprised the seven nothern provinces which were united since 1579 in their struggle for independence from Spanish rule. Thus, the Dutch were preoccupied with the crisis conditions imposed by the war, and matters of defense and military expediency were sure to have high priority in spite of cost. Whatever the conditions, Dutch prag-

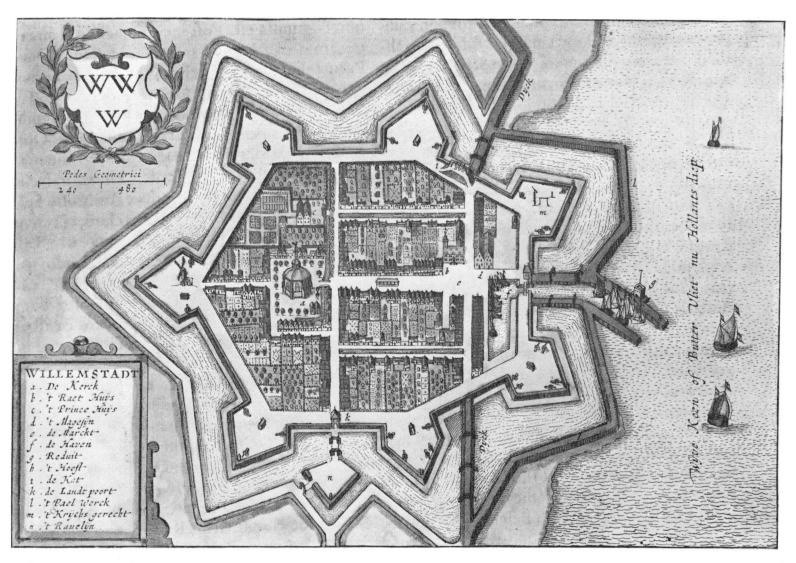

WILLEMSTADT

a . De Kerck
b . 't Raet Huys
c . 't Prince Huys
d . 't Magesijn
e . de Marckt
f . de Haven
g . Reduit
h . 't Hoeft
i . de Kat
k . de Lande poort
l . 't Bael Werck
m . 't Krijchs gerecht
n . 't Rauelyn

37. Zuerius van Boxhorn, *plan of Willemstad, 1632*

matism and sense of economy would not discount useful theory from whichever directions it came; this may account for the appearance in the Netherlands of a number of cities with utopian linkages. The theoretical trappings, however, were less important than the usefulness of the forms for a nation under seige. Practice rather than theory was the stimulus for Renaissance planning in sixteenth-century Netherlands. "Their local rulers, on the whole, adopted the attitude not of the petty despot [or the dogmatic theorist] but of the shrewd administrator," according to Gerald Burke; "their towns were centres of commercial and industrial activity, not monuments to the vanity of a dictator."[18]

Because land was such a valuable commodity, the Dutch councils in founding cities were most concerned with its optimum use and were little given to the risks of experimentation in its development. Nor did Dutch individualism, even in an atmosphere dominated by the emergencies of war, succumb to Baroque autocracy or seek to build physical environments glorifying it. Nevertheless, there are two examples of Dutch town building with clear ties to the planned circular cities of Renaissance ideal city theory that to a remarkable extent managed transplanting to Dutch soil: Willemstad and Coevorden.

Willemstad, the earlier of the two, had the orthogonal and axial symmetry of many of the plans of Renaissance theorists (fig. 37). The site had originally been chosen in 1565 for the agricultural town of Ruigenhil to serve the people settling in a new polder on the lands of Brabant owned by the Marquis of Bergen op Zoom. In due course these lands became the property of William the Silent, who recognized the strategic position of the site and in 1583 ordered the town redeveloped as a fortified place, renamed Willemstad. But it was Maurice of Nassau, William's son, under whom the city's new development took place (his father had been assassinated in 1584). With Maurice's patronage Willemstad was to become a major

strongpoint in the defensive network of that part of Europe.

The symbolism of the ideal city tradition was not antithetical to the Dutch personality; Willemstad demonstrated a taste for it. For the Dutch, the number seven had special significance: besides its reputation as a lucky integer in the contemporary magic of numbers (Alberti believed in this as well), there was also the coincidence of the seven united provinces which originally declared their independence from Spain in 1581. Dutch cities with seven bastions were a reminder of this symbolism and its associated magic.[19] Willemstad was one of them, a city with an odd rather than even number of sides, an unusual occurrence in contemporary ideal city theory and practice. Like the rest of the Renaissance world, the Dutch combined rationality with an element of the magical. But under most circumstances they managed to keep the mystical comfortably in check.

The city's seven-bastioned walls, designed by the engineer Adriaan Anthonisz from Alkmaarse and begun by William the Silent's order but finished by his son, combined earthen parapets and bastions facing a wide ditch. (Willemstad also had an additional protective device: its defenders could flood the surrounding land and did so successfully during the siege of 1793.) There were two gateways leading out from the city, one toward the land, the other toward the waterway.[20] Within the city's walls the plan was symmetrical on either side of the northeast-southwest alignment of the main street (oriented to the line of the waterway, not the cosmos), which was generously wide and lined with substantial but modest two-story houses. This street led to a large square open space, not the town square, however, which was a somewhat indeterminate area at the main street's northeast end, but a moated and landscaped enclave where a brick octagonal church was built (with central plan implications). The city's scale was modest, domestic, and served well the practical purposes William had in

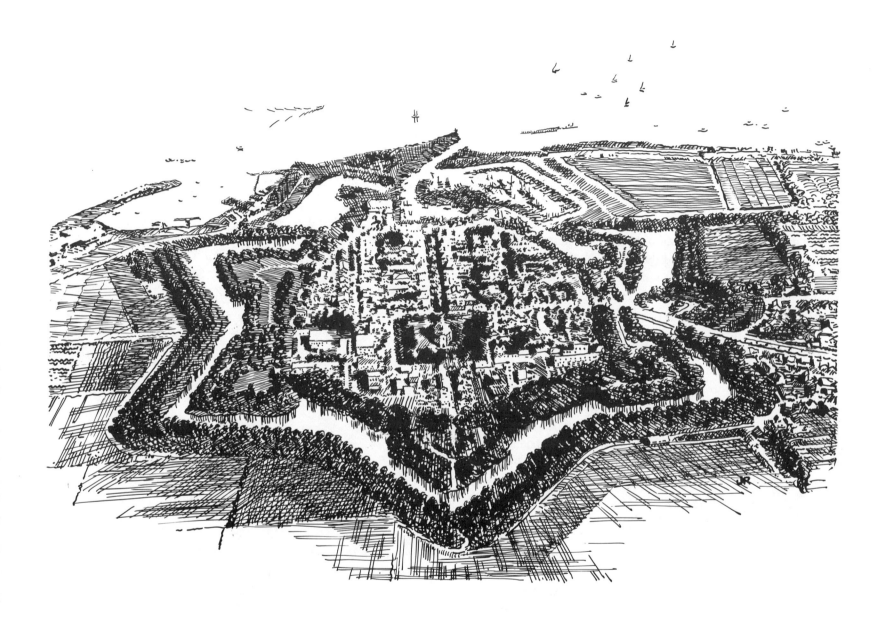

38. Willemstad (Rohrer)

mind when he envisioned the city's role in the country's defense. Willemstad was, as Burke notes, "a neat little essay in Renaissance idealism," with static limits imposed on its future growth by the kind of plan selected for it.

The strategic importance of Willemstad continued into the early twentieth century, though after World War I it declined into relative obscurity, being dropped as a unit in Dutch defense in 1926. But its static state, a city immobilized by its walls and restricted from contiguous development, saved it for its present role as a protected and picturesque national monument in a green open space of trails and boating routes (fig. 38). This preservation, and the adjoining development of the new Volkerak-dam with one of the largest locks in Europe, have brought new life to the city.[21] This comes at a time when an appreciation of Willemstad's past has emerged, suggesting that it has a more sympathetic future than many other cities sharing its ideological past.

Coevorden's rebuilding closed the century and brought the Netherlands its most extravagant experiment with ideal city form. The city, located in the border area with Germany, received town privileges in the early twelfth century. The Spanish totally destroyed it during the war for independence in 1592. But the Dutch, recognizing its advantageous location, proceeded with its rebuilding from 1597 to 1601 in what would be the latest military planning technology, a radioconcentric fortress town. There is no specific evidence of who or what was its inspiration. But the Dutch, already familiar with the theoretical and technical planning literature coming out of Italy and elsewhere and with its nearby Spanish applications, had demonstrated their ability to adapt these lessons to their own needs at Willemstad. Coevorden extended that experience to a more sophisticated level, embracing fully the mannerisms of ideal city theory for the rebuilding of this border strongpoint.

39. *Plan of Coevorden*

Modifying the symbols to reflect their own experience, the Dutch again chose seven-sided encircling walls connected to the town's central square and marketplace by radial streets (fig. 39). The presence of remains from the earlier city required some altering of what might otherwise have been perfect symmetry; there were only five of these radial connectors to the walls, the other two routes omitted to accommodate the original castle and its moated enclosure.* In spite of the violence the presence of the castle did to the symmetry of their ideal plan, the Dutch sense of economy did not permit its replacement

* Recently the castle was restored for museum purposes.

simply for the sake of regularity. Instead, they built the new city with the castle in a peripheral location in an otherwise idealized composition. With time, further refinements gave Coevorden a brilliant outer ring of bastions, scarps, lunettes, glacis, and ditches, an impressive reminder that even Dutch stolidity could succumb to the extravagances of the art and mathematics of the cosmic city when such elegance might serve a useful purpose.[22]

But Coevorden, like Willemstad, has lost its strategic importance; it has become simply a provincial town. Most of its elaborate star-shaped fortifications, which were still in place into the nineteenth century, are now leveled or filled in to permit typical urban processes of growth and change to take place, free from the plan's earlier constraints. The Dutch had only limited patience with forcing peaceful civilian life into a rigid theoretical form. Perhaps, also, they recognized that a small frugal nation had limits on its ability to preserve Renaissance ideal cities, retaining Willemstad but releasing Coevorden to develop along more conventional lines. One can regret the loss of Coevorden's earlier formal purity, yet appreciate the lively commercial city of today which enjoys extensive greenbelts and waterways threading through its form, remnants of the lines of fortification that once proclaimed Coevorden to be the Netherlands' only radioconcentric cosmic city.

Though the Renaissance moved also into France, Germany, and England, the influence of its ideal city theories on those countries through the sixteenth century was selective. France would seem entirely eligible for indulging in such schemes, having a strong centralized government to direct them and national resources for their support. But only a few such plans were realized: as a response to Spanish pressures in her northern border areas, France in 1545 built three fortress cities which reflected the influx of Renaissance ideas coming north out of Italy.

By order of Francis I, Vitry-le-François was rebuilt on a new orthogonal plan in the area east of Paris after its destruction by the armies of Charles V. It was to be France's first Renaissance city. Its designer, an Italian engineer/architect from Bologna, Girolamo Marini, was obviously unable to overcome the more conservative urban views of his client (fig. 40). Rather than

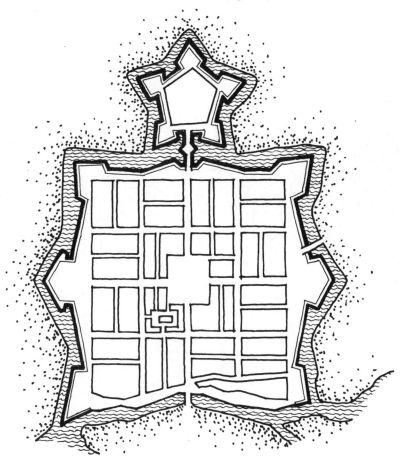

40. *Plan of Vitry-le-François*

following Italian fashions, he kept to French rectangular bastide traditions, producing little more than a stylized version of those medieval rectangular forms, only moderately adjusted to fit prevailing principles of military engineering.[23]

Villefranche-sur-Meuse's radial plan suggested more possibilities for applying ideal city concepts, with an overall character almost identical to that of Marienbourg (fig. 41). But any future it might have had as a model for others to admire and follow was blighted by subsequent events which destroyed its military purpose. Located on France's northern border, it was poorly situated for any function other than a military one, and

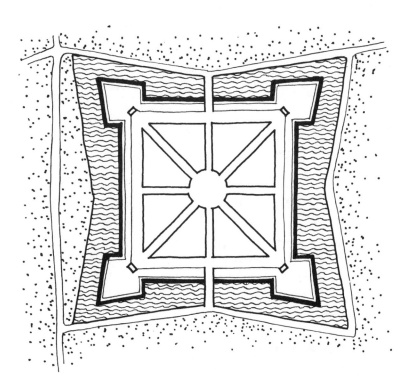

41. *Plan of Villefranche-sur-Meuse, 1650*

border changes were soon to supersede it. By order of the king, it lost its fortifications and military status, to molder into a future of no consequence for theory or practice in French urban experience.

Finally, there was Rocroi, whose initial fortification work, like that of the others, was begun in 1545. It also had a radial plan which, when combined with its pentagonal outline, was to be a more daring employment by the French of Italian ideal city formal concepts (fig. 42). Located only a short distance south of both Marienbourg and Philippeville, it was based on a similar radial plan, and all three towns may indeed have acted as precedent and inspiration for each other during the years of their struggling development. Their present-day appearances are all much alike, Philippeville being the only one to lose the stricture of its walls and to expand modestly beyond their original alignment. In spite of France's apparent eligibility for extravagant employment of ideal city models, initial gestures remained tentative. The planned circular city awaited the seventeenth century before it came more fully alive in France.

Germany could also have been expected to share in utopian circular city plans, given her national penchant for cerebral speculations and ritualized organizational approaches to problem solving. The country had a considerable record of medieval bastide experience on which such activity might have been built, as well as her own theorists following Italian precedent. Albrecht Dürer in 1527 had designed an ideal city, but showed no interest in the radial or circular aspects of Italian concepts. Instead, he offered a strictly orthogonal solution to the utopian ideal, a square in outline and internal organization with L-shaped blocks separated by straight streets. It is a design that appears to owe nothing to a hundred years of Italian theorizing except the coincidence of their pursuit of the same utopia. As has already been noted, Daniel Speckle responded more directly to Italian inspiration with his polygonal and radial city.

42. *Plan of Rocroi, 1650*

glish stirrings in the arts, both architecture and the forms of the city would await the seventeenth century for positive responses to Renaissance influences. But even if the English had not been out of step in time, it is likely they would have been gingerly in handling the ideal city mystique. As Gutkind has written:

England's Renaissance has produced Utopias but no Ideal Cities. Unlike Italy, France, and Germany, she never translated the vision of her illustrious dreamers into designs which would present the new ideas in a tangible form; still less did she think of building a Palma Nova, a Henrichemont, or a Freudenstadt. For her the written word

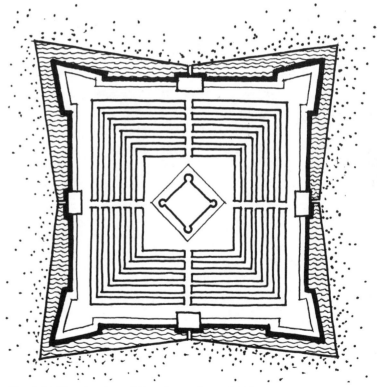

43. *Schickhardt, plan of Freudenstadt, c. 1600*

But this failed to be reciprocated in any way by German practice, at least in the sixteenth century. An ideal city was built, Freudenstadt in southwest Germany, but its plan adhered almost literally to Dürer's concept. Designed by the architect Heinrich Schickhardt (1558–1634), it closed the century as Germany's only experiment in ideal city planning, entirely aloof from any circularity (fig. 43).

England came late to the Renaissance. Though Thomas More had already set his own standards in his *Utopia* of 1516 (his city "in fashion almost four-square") and there were En-was potent enough to reflect the spirit of the time. She shied away from expressing in contemporary language of form the concept of a city as a whole. Latin and Germanic speculation were alien to the tarrying pragmatism of England. Only what was practically possible, what could be fitted into the existing structures of towns and cities without a fundamental transformation, was attempted.[24]

It rounds out the record nicely to return to Italy where the Renaissance began, since there the Renaissance chapter of the planned circular city is concluded. After 1600 the social and political atmosphere of Europe changed, establishing new circumstances and rationale for life and for the arts it produced. But in the sixteenth century's closing years the Italians, who had initiated much of the era's urban theory, were at last to fill out the record with the most complete and finest of the planned circular cities.

Palmanova* had a sponsor with the necessary credentials for such aspirations: the Venetian Republic with its great commercial wealth, overseas possessions, and autocratic government. The rulers of the republic through the sixteenth century had felt apprehensions about the defense of its eastern borders against Austrian and Turkish threats. They concluded that a powerful citadel located in the flatlands northeast of Venice (the Friuli Plain) would be best suited for securing the area, and on 7 October 1593 construction began at the chosen site with appropriate ceremonies. (The date also marked the anniversary of the Battle of Lepanto in 1571 in which the Turks were decisively defeated by an allied fleet that included the

Venetians.) The Venetian goals from the beginning were ambitious: to build the world's largest and most powerful fortress. It was to be a city with a system of twelve bastions, each with accessory fortified works, but economics intervened to reduce their number to the nine we know today. Even with its reduced circumstances, for its times Palmanova was to be the largest of Europe's fortress cities.[25]

Popular tradition has it that Palmanova was designed by Vincenzo Scamozzi, who, as already noted, was a contributor to ideal planning theory. Certainly the plan for the city as finally accepted had strong ties with the considerable theoretical and technical literature that preceded it from Alberti and Filarete onward, and Scamozzi is known to have been active at the time when actual construction began on the city (frontispiece and fig. 44). Nevertheless, substantial evidence suggests others were the city's engineers and designers, especially Giulio Savorgnano, who was then the "ruling dean" of Venetian military architects, or his assistant Bonaiuto Lorini.[26]

Maria Giuffrè supports Lorini as a possible designer, noting that he was an engineer in the same office with Scamozzi and, according to a document now in the State Archives in Venice, was present at the meeting on 16 October 1593 during which it was decided to begin work on Palmanova. In this document, neither Scamozzi nor Savorgnano is mentioned. Giuffrè also mentions Savorgnano and Marcantonio Montinengo as possible contributors, with Savorgnano designing the plan of the fortress while Montinengo was said to have outlined it on the ground and modified it.[27] Mario Morini, however, concludes that Savorgnano and Montinengo were the designers, with Scamozzi assigned responsibility for the cathedral and gates.[28] The number of preliminary plans for Palmanova that still exist suggests the variety of designers participating in what was obviously a major construction project for the republic, one whose design would not be casually determined. But whoever

---

* Originally named Palma; the name Palmanova, currently in use, has been employed since the mid-1600s. Documents and foreign charts also refer to it as Nova Palma, Palma Nuova, and Palma Nova (A. Visentin and O. Piani, *Guida di Palmanova*, p. 16).

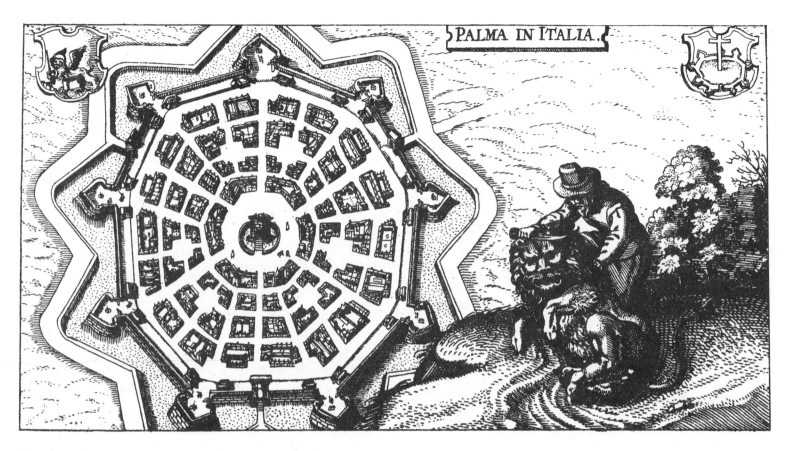

44. Plan of Palmanova (engraving by Daniel Meisner, 1630)

the author or authors, the antecedents of the city are clear enough: planned circular ideal cities of the Renaissance, adapted for the realities of late sixteenth-century warfare. The results were to be the most complete and perfect of the genre.

Among several anonymous designs for the Palma project which have survived, [one] represents the military ideal in its most frigidly functional severity. Nine master streets depart from the corners of the nine-sided central piazza and lead straight for their respective bastions. Secondary streets lead toward curtain centers, but are cut off from them, as well as from the piazza, by building strips. In his overwhelming concern for the plan's utilitarian, military aspects, the designer did not even bother to provide his city with gates. Savorgnano might well have thought in these terms, for we are told that the gates on his lost master model for the city were hidden in the shadows of bastions and, thus, were offset from the street system. The extreme and almost crude functionalism of such designs must have shocked Marcantonio Barbaro, the project's first general supervisor, who was a lawyer, humanist, and friend of such men as Veronese, Palladio, and Scamozzi.[29] [Horst de la Croix]

Palmanova's preliminary plans and the one on which it eventually developed are different in some significant ways. Scamozzi claimed that in his work there "he did many things too numerous to mention," which de la Croix thinks may mean that he as an architect had the opportunity to alter things previously based on military considerations and which "must have shocked Barbaro." "In effect," says de la Croix, "Palma the fortress was emasculated in a futile attempt to create Palma the city."[30] Differences do appear in the final plan which may have added to the livability of the city at the cost of military convention. Certainly the breaking of direct access from all but three of the bastions to the central square would have been cause for shock among the military engineers. But in so doing, by relieving the mechanical monotony of the original fan-shaped grids, introducing a series of peripheral neighborhood squares, and providing different approach alignments to the central square with its somewhat more clearly perceived hexagonal shape, the built plan offered a more flexible manipulation of the inevitable radioconcentric rigidities.

The plan focused on the city square, which was to have had a fortress tower that was never built. Vitruvius would have wanted a temple and Alberti a palace; Giocondo visualized a domed centrally-planned building for the greatest Renaissance harmony between architecture and city. At least the tower would have given three-dimensional prominence to this key point in Palmanova's plan instead of the vacuum that was left in its absence. Of the six streets radiating from the square, three led to the city gates, the others stopped at the walls. An additional twelve streets also lead to the walls but commenced only at the innermost of the city's four circumferential streets; six of them bisected each of the city's neighborhood squares. The walls were a single line of heavy masonry-faced earth-filled bastions and curtains, broken only by the three handsome Scamozzi gates. A ditch followed the wall line to separate the city entirely from its surrounding fields, cleared and open for military efficiency. These fortifications were considered to represent the highest standard of the day for Renaissance military design.

Progress in the city's construction went slowly, taking some twenty years for the plan to be realized. People were not easily attracted to live in Palmanova, in spite of government encouragements, and the technology of the works slowed the pace of

45. *Plan of Palmanova, 1851*

development as well. Landslides were a serious problem because of shifting in the masses of fill required for the ramparts; this continued to plague the engineers for decades. Further work was required, too, as military engineering itself responded to new theory and conditions. The single line of ramparts was soon seen as insufficient, and additional barriers were built beyond the line of the ditch. These ravelins and glacis added further splendor to Palmanova's outer limits, which received their final form from Napoleon in the nineteenth century through restoration and further modernization with a line of added lunettes (fig. 45). Of course these also served to further encase the inner city, dwarfed by its surrounding expanse of construction and earthworks.

Perhaps because of the great expectations that the republic had for its fortress city, and the elaborate defenses that resulted, Palmanova's history has been relatively quiet. At least during the time that the republic continued its rule, the city never faced a siege, a testimonial to the intimidating effect its presence had on both the Turks and Austrians. But in 1797 it was briefly occupied by the Austrians, followed a few days later with a victorious entry into the city by the French, who ended its 204-year history of Venetian control. Becoming a part of the new Italian kingdom in 1866, the city was declared by the national government in 1883 no longer to have fortress status, though it would continue to be used as a garrison town. In 1960 it was declared a national monument, and like Willemstad now enjoys whatever status that implies in local and national policy.[31]

Palmanova's present-day pace is a provincial one (fig. 46). The central square remains open, occupied only by a fine flagpole that is quite lost in the vast vacuum of the central square bordered by trees and statues (general superintendents of the past). The surrounding buildings include the cathedral (1605–36), the city hall (1598, originally the general superintendent's residence), and the former palace of the governor of armaments (1613), all with an unpretentious but suitable presence today. The bulk of the city is made up of modest two- and three-story masonry construction with contiguous facades lining the streets; much of this earlier construction suffered from the bombardments of twentieth-century wars.

Modifications have taken place through the years that have somewhat altered the city's plan, usually weakening it. Continuity of some of the concentric streets has been broken; the street adjacent to the walls has been built over; of the six neighborhood squares only one exists in its entirety, two others in part. Violence has also been done to the architectural fabric of the city. But the dormant state of its economy, and perhaps the very nature of the city's plan with its built-in resistance to change, have inhibited new development, thus avoiding some of the worst outrages that modern construction or destruction can bring to a historical ambiance. Like Willemstad, Palmanova lies enclosed within its walls, quietly secure in an agricultural landscape that still permits distant vistas of this special monument whose patterns and forms give eloquent testimony to the impact of Renaissance ideal city concepts.

As we have seen from their writings and designs, Renaissance theorists continued the speculations about the nature of the ideal city, a line of inquiry whose strands reached back through medieval and Classical times to earliest inspiration. Although the Renaissance relied on the theoretical abstracts of perfect beauty rather than on cosmic order transposed to an earthbound setting or specifications for a *Civitas Dei*, the urban paragon remained the planned circular city. But the discussion, in spite of the numbers of investigators it attracted in the fifteenth and sixteenth centuries, remained largely preoccupied with the circular city's planimetrics. Rarely did the theo-

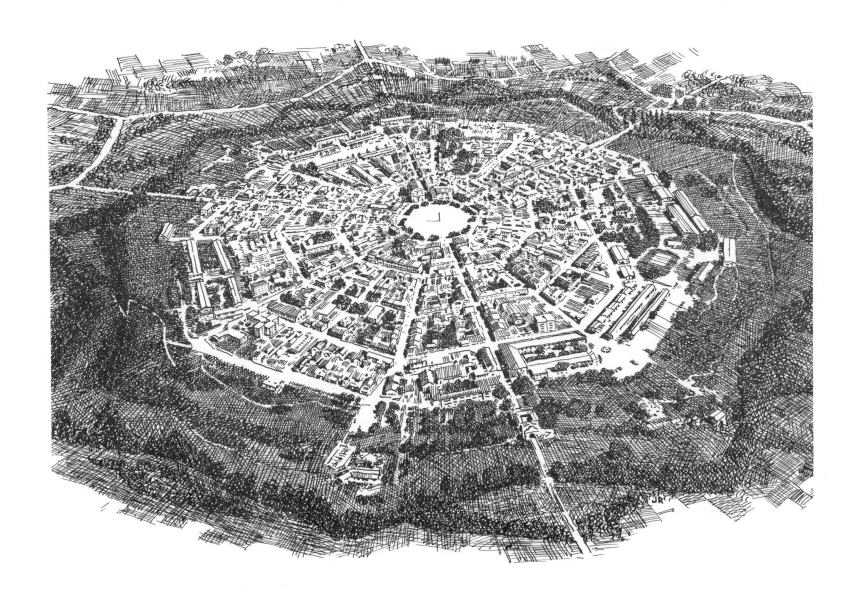

46. *Palmanova (Rohrer)*

rists adventure beyond the ritual of two-dimensional geometry in their search for an urban prescription for beauty.

More serious was their neglect of content. Only occasionally were plans modified toward the goal of improved lives as well as forms. Speckle's work might include some evidence of such an extended awareness; Palmanova's plan has adjustments that appear to reflect such a concern. But the concept of the ideal city on the whole remained dominantly skewed to goals of plan patterns rather than human content. Little was allowed to interrupt the rituals and rigidities of the planned circular city.

Yet, as an aspect of Renaissance humanism, the implication of concern for betterment of human life was there—the true ideal city—a potential which, had the Renaissance been allowed to run its course, might have led to a more complete weaving of the abstracts of the ideal city with a happier social order. But any such realization was not to be. In part, this was due to the thinkers themselves, inadequately prepared for or encouraged toward such an adventure. But, more importantly, the times were to move beyond them: the Renaissance was subverted by the autocratic policies of the Baroque state, whose values were little inclined toward the philosophical concerns of utopians except for an appreciation of the facility with which their ideal city forms could be exploited for the state's own purposes.

The Renaissance did build a number of planned circular cities which satisfied ideal environmental visions: streets, buildings, open spaces, and outlines that to the observer matched utopian formulas. But they were shells that created a formal vocabulary all too easy for others to transpose for quite different uses. Indeed, as the sixteenth century discovered and the seventeenth and eighteenth centuries would fully demonstrate, the idealized circular city form could be readily manipulated. Instead of a search for abstract beauty and alternatives to the present order, the city's shell would be exploited for the technologies of the military engineer and for locking in the rigidities of the existing system. The fate of the ideal city was an index of the vulnerability of the Renaissance itself; its tradition of humanism was easily overcome by more powerful and cynical forces, the sacred succumbing to the profane. Thus, the Renaissance city in the round was transformed into the Baroque star-shaped ramparted fortress, brilliant in its patterns but indifferent to the life of its residents and calculatedly cold in its preoccupations with the aggressions and suppressions of the monarch and the state.

VI. Baroque Circular Cities: Seventeenth and Eighteenth Centuries

THE RENAISSANCE PRINCE, representing a central focus for the emerging national state, laid social and political foundations for the Baroque monarchy that followed. The roving medieval court, tenuously exerting its jurisdiction over the rivalries of feudalism, had been replaced by the authority of the prince and his move toward a permanent capital to house national institutions. Lacking any effective precedent for checking his authority once it had been established, the process of centralization advanced with a kind of inexorable force toward an inevitable conclusion—the ultimate absolutism of the Baroque monarch. Italy and Central Europe would continue in their multiplicity of political divisions. But even there Baroque environmental and social trappings were admired and emulated, though the resources for their support would be considerably more constrained and local.

What evolved was an aristocratic society that interpreted the burdens of governing as requiring its own aggrandizement. Its position, granted by heavenly endowment, was buttressed by institutions of society and state: the church, the academy, the army, the bureaucracy. It has been said about that paradigm of Baroque autocracy, Louis XIV, and Versailles, the setting he created for himself, that Louis needed not another place to live but a means for reaffirming the splendors of France and of his reign in the eyes of his people and the world. Versailles was no self-serving caprice but the calculated response of a Baroque monarch to his responsibilities.

Any incipient humanism of the Renaissance would of course find no place in such a climate. One king, one faith, one discipline, one doctrine, one standard: it was a tyranny of mind and spirit in which whatever individualized speculation the Renaissance had achieved would be required to give way before the ever-encroaching controls and repressions of the state. Focus shifted from individualized utopian speculations to dictated collective values, coalescing about the figure of the monarch.

Collectivism was also encouraged in other ways. The years spanning the end of the sixteenth and beginning of the seventeenth century were unsettled ones, mutilated by religious and political rivalries, aggressions, and attendant cruelties and destruction. The army, with its arsenal of increasingly versatile armaments, was to become a permanent feature in national life. Its support during peacetime and in war would be a major national responsibility. Beyond its military role in defending the nation's interests abroad, the army of course also served to maintain the position, prestige, and privileges of the monarchy at home.

Cities in such circumstances were to be shaped by a period of bold development. They had the enormous advantage of sponsorship by a highly centralized state with the authority, willingness, and resources to plan and build extravagantly. The city, representing the most ambitious of the environmental arts, would thus be an ideal medium through which the mon-

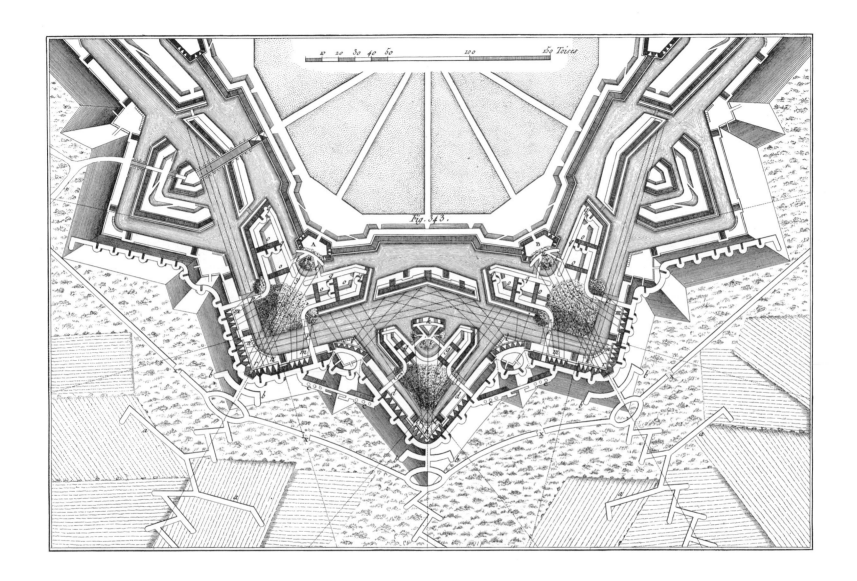

Fig. 343.

47. *Military engineering for an eighteenth-century fortress city*

archy could express its values, both in the remodeling and expansion of existing cities (the more usual means) and in the construction of new ones. But a shift in priorities had also crystallized. Defense would become a central theme of both theorists and builders. Even the nature of site selection would be affected; discounted were the old Vitruvian standards calling for sites that were "high and free from clouds and hoar frost" and that avoided marshy neighborhoods. The obverse conditions, while inconvenient to residents, earned favor for the nuisance they would be to an invading army in its movement of troops and deployment of heavy guns and equipment.[1] Once located, the city required fortifications shaped to new standards evolving out of the changing nature of warfare (figs. 47, 48). These investments exceeded local resources and required dependence on the national government and its treasury, binding the city and its people more tightly into the authoritarian web of the Baroque state.

The forms *within* the city were also refashioned by its new responsibilities as a theater for Baroque society, expressive of esthetics based on formality, grandeur, coordination, and visual perspective and drama. The sumptuous palaces of the aristocracy, the major buildings of the bureaucracy, the arsenal and barracks, the opera house, churches, and gardens: all required a place within a coordinated design, dominated by geometry, in which axial and fan-patterned avenues and boulevards, public squares, uniform facades and building heights, landscape, and street embellishments were manipulated to satisfy Baroque egocentricities. These were cities in which people were reduced to spectators in their affirmation of the power, splendor, and permanence of the existing order. The Baroque elite required complementary forms in their cities in which to play out their spectacles. Sébastien le Prestre de Vauban, who codified the new design standards for the Baroque fortress city, also saw the myopia of this approach. Toward the end of his life he was to write his master, Louis XIV, "Compelled by my conscience, I feel obliged to tell your Majesty that in the very many cities that we have built the life and the life conditions of the inhabitants, of those people who carried and still carry the heaviest burdens of the kingdom, were always neglected and not taken into account."[2]

The Baroque monarchy recognized the ways in which its own position could be buttressed by adaptations of circular city traditions. The structured order of such cities was embraced for its ability to reaffirm the presence and power of the monarchy in the eyes and minds of the people. And when more direct means for control were required, the circular city model contributed handily to the maneuverability of the local garrison. Hardly ever would the forms of seventeenth- and eighteenth-century cities in the round be expected to carry any of the philosophical content which at one time provided that concept with its unique panache.

It was for the service of this Baroque value system that the vocabulary of the Renaissance ideal city found itself inadvertently requisitioned. Even before the seventeenth century its own formal biases had allowed it to be manipulated by those who would exploit it for pragmatic ends. Baroque planners would extend that subversion, especially in their manipulation of the planned circular city in the service of a central preoccupation: the city's defense. The role of the theorist was subsumed under the umbrella of the military engineer. Indeed, the theorist and engineer had become one, following a trend already established in the Renaissance and not to be broken until the late eighteenth century and the disintegration of Baroque society. Thus, the last half of the sixteenth century had seen publication of three treatises that summarized the conventional wisdom of the time: Pietro Cataneo's *I quattro primi libri di architettura* (1554), Girolamo Maggi's *Della fortificazione delle città* (1564), and Francesco de Marchi's *Della*

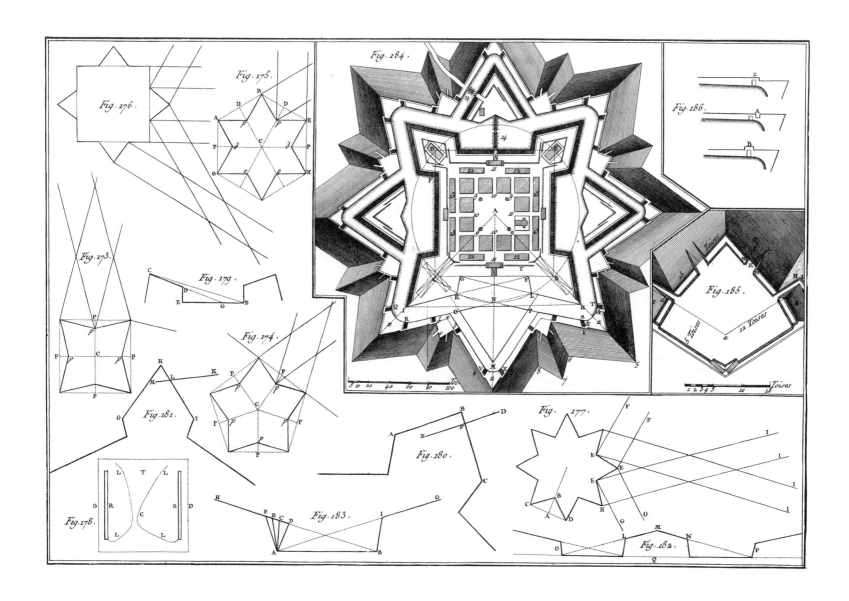

48. *Eighteenth-century military engineering*

architettura militare (1599). Even their titles set the trend, the latter two emphasizing military preparedness to the exclusion of other concerns. The direction of seventeenth-century planning had therefore been securely set by what had gone before: the city was to be a fortress, whether by remodeling an existing urban base or laying out a new one. The bellwether was military science, and all other aspects of urban design were subordinate to its concerns. As at Palmanova, the vast horizontal radiating sprawl of fortifications often exceeded in area the modest town which they enclosed in their grip. The result was dazzling formal brilliance, but a static ritual, frozen in a preconceived order, mechanically indifferent to varying conditions

49. *Sardi, ideal city*

of site and climate, in which opportunities for creative response to growth and change had been locked out of the city's future.

Interest in Vitruvius continued in the seventeenth and eighteenth centuries; new editions of his books were issued, though the impact of his message was lost in the welter of military calculations. Even his recommendations for the city's radial street organization were modified by more recent military developments. Improved firepower and artillery range required the moving of the defensive perimeter farther out from the city. Walls and bastions were supplemented by lunettes and their assorted ditches and glacis, advance stations to confront the attackers and repel them well short of the city's walls. Thus, supplying the bastions—a function for which the radial street plan had been especially effective—was no longer so pressing a priority. This permitted the Baroque city's designers the convenience of the more practical grid plan for the city's interior areas, which simplified property assignments and enhanced development potentials. Only the Vitruvian polygonal perimeter continued to enjoy currency in the face of Baroque military pragmatics.

The Baroque City Theorists

The theoretical literature of the Baroque centuries is a reaffirmation of these military biases, though certain national personality traits may suggest the authors' origins as they developed their approaches to the city. Centrally and symmetrically organized, the city is the body clasped tightly in the ring of its defenses. These stellar complexities, usually polygonal in alignment, make brilliant two-dimensional plan patterns and entirely dominate their city's modest kernel. Yet some Baroque theorists, overshadowed as they were by military priorities, lin-

50. *Dilich, ideal cities*

gered tenuously over peripheral elements of ideal city memory: an occasional reference to the quality of human life within the city as well as its preservation behind defensive walls; provision for some open space to relieve the city's density; and even sympathy for the poor and their general neglect by the Baroque establishment.

Pietro Sardi, a seventeenth-century Italian theorist, published works which had recommendations characteristic of a transitional fortress scheme (*Corona imperiale dell'architettura militare*, Venice, 1617; and *Corno dogale dell'architettura militare*, Venice, 1639). Within his circular city he retained a system of radial streets leading out to the battlements but also linking the city's main square with a series of smaller peripheral squares (fig. 49). In addition, besides generalized principles for building the fortress city, he included considerations for locating within it the governor's palace, residential areas, churches, military quarters and storage facilities, and hospitals. Sardi managed to see his city for more than its defensive potential. But the resulting pattern was mechanical and rigid, its core fragmented into inconvenient and often awkwardly-shaped building blocks with much of the city's buildable area lost to circulation requirements.

Although previously the Italians had taken the major initiative in idealizations of the city, in the seventeenth and eighteenth centuries this role was to be assumed by others. Germans were particularly active, perhaps a mark of their nature and also of the more secure hold that Italian influences had now established in their environmental arts. Wilhelm Schäfer (who wrote under the *nom de plume* of Dilich) was one such figure. His *Peribologia oder Bericht von Vestungs Gebauden* (Frankfurt, 1640) included urban proposals that were strongly circular and radial in their planning approach. He provided some four hundred plan etchings much in the manner of Palmanova or Speckle's ideal city, including some curious efforts to apply his radioconcentric plans to sites whose seashore or

51. *Rimpler, ideal city*

river locations precluded the total symmetry of an idealized plan (fig. 50). The proposals offer remarkably little concession to locational circumstances and affirm the rigidity of Dilich's thinking. His book is evidence of the extent to which the Italians had influenced him in his abandonment of the square city traditions of his fellow nationals such as Dürer or Schickardt.

On the other hand, George Rimpler, born in Leipzig in 1635, combined circular and square cities, presumably for the advantages of each, with an approach that was similar to that of Dürer, only gentler. His book, *Kriegs-Baukunst* (1671), offered an ideal city with a strictly orthogonal urban core surrounded by additional rectangular streets and blocks whose perimeter was adjusted to an almost circular outline bounded by star-shaped ramparts (fig. 51). However, Rimpler's plan for Ansbach, a Bavarian provincial capital which he assisted in planning, was entirely loyal to the Freudenstadt square city model. So was L. Christoph Sturm's ideal city plan which he published in 1719 in *Architectura civilis-militaris*. Its static approach was softened somewhat by a continuous sequence of parks paralleling the interior line of the fortifying walls.

The bias among German Baroque theorists was thus toward their own Renaissance antecedents; they were aware of the circular city theories of the Italians but for German purposes were content to use more traditional planning forms. Only in the special case of Karlsruhe* do we find any significant German employment of a radioconcentric city plan, the absence of peripheral fortification lines opening the city's radials unendingly to the broad plane of its site in the Rhine Valley.

The French displayed no reluctance in observing Italian precedent. The seventeenth century opened with Jacques Perret's *Des fortifications et artifices d'architecture et perspective*

---

* Its two imitators, Neustrelitz (Mecklenburg, 1726) and Karlsruhe (Silesia, 1743), are only pale shadows of their prototype.

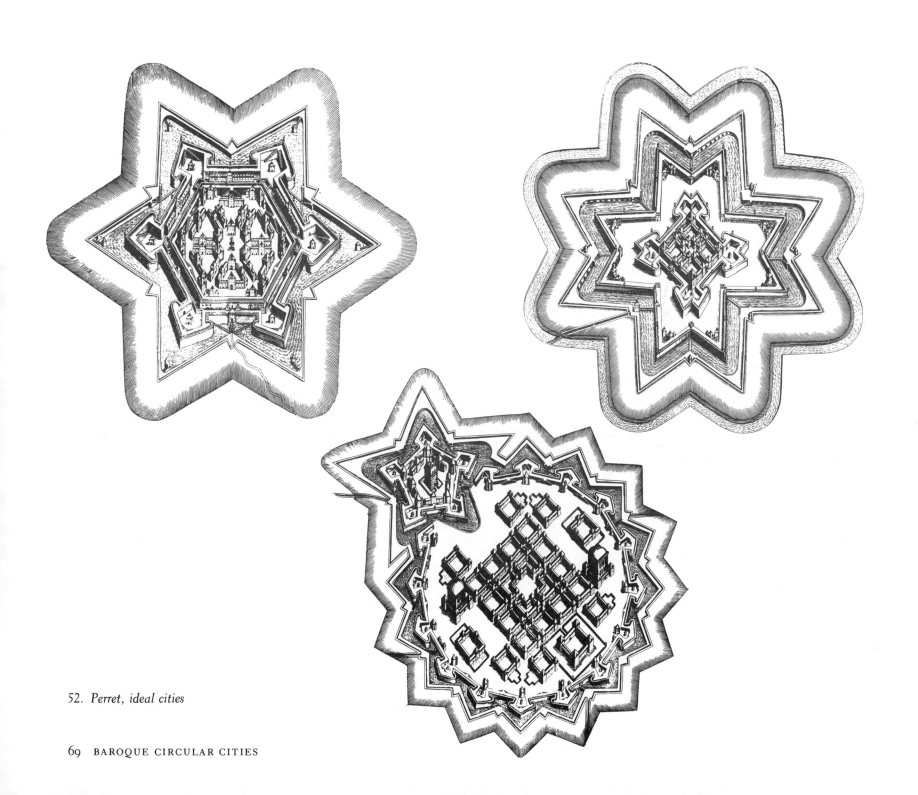

52. Perret, *ideal cities*

(Paris, 1601), which presented five different ideal city proposals, each one a variation on circular city themes (fig. 52). The proposals began with relatively modest-scale four-, five-, and six-pointed star plans with glacis, ditches, and ramparts. Their enclosed spaces were each developed with symmetrically-arranged multiple-story buildings, the corners of their long facades marked by tall towers. The final two designs in the book were variations on circular city themes, multi-angled perimeters following a circular alignment broken only by a star-shaped citadel which had been incorporated into the line of the fortifications. One of these circular cities was entirely radial, emanating from an octagonal city square in which rose, in the manner of Palmanova's plan, a ten-story building that combined the governor's palace with the city bureaucracy. Arcaded market squares, public parks, high density housing, and commercial and storage buildings made up the balance of the plan. The other ideal city was of similar high-density construction but composed on a strictly orthogonal plan with, however, a rather generous amount of open space as transition between the straight lines of the streets and the circle of the multi-bastioned walls. Perret's plans all indicate tightly codified and ritualized exercises with only minimal consideration for the nature and needs of urban life.

Jean Errard de Bar-le-Duc (1554-1610) was a contemporary of Perret and an engineer for Henry IV. The author of *La Fortification demontrée et réduicte en art* (Paris, 1620), he exercised his interest in ideal city concepts by providing a range of axially-ordered interpretations of polygons with sides variously numbered from three to twelve (fig. 53). Errard's proposals were about equally divided between radial or orthogonal plans, although when he was working with the more specific circumstances of proposals for port cities he chose the orthogonal. Gutkind notes an earlier manuscript by Errard, *De la fortification* (1604), preserved in the Bibliothèque Nationale of Paris, in which his ideal city plans, except for one radial scheme, are all tediously based on an orthogonal layout.[3]

The French were to dominate European city and fortification design from the second half of the seventeenth century onward, not through the theoretical rituals of Perret or Errand but in the combination of theory and practice represented by the career of Sébastien le Prestre de Vauban (1633–1707). As Louis XIV's premier military engineer, he built a dramatic record of achievement with credit for remodeling more than 160 fortresses as well as building 30 new ones, directing 53 sieges, and involvement in nearly 50 battles.[4] Obviously a man of substance and action in the military affairs of Baroque France, he also expanded his influence by publications; his *Manière de fortifier* (Amsterdam, 1689) and *Essais sur la fortification* (Paris, 1739) provided his contemporaries and the eighteenth century as well with handbooks on the science of fortress design.

Vauban's career included both fortification and city planning; he considered them to be symbiotic, of course, but each requiring its own special skills and insight. Even though he was more interested in the city's defensive periphery, he was not insensitive to the inner city and its life, and to a remarkable degree for his times was sympathetic with the common people of his cities. Note has already been made of his letter to Louis XIV, expressing this concern. Further, in his *Projet d'une dîme royale* (1707) he wrote that "what is erroneously called the scum of the people" deserves on the contrary the most serious attention of the "heavenly king," and he added, "These masses are . . . very important because of their number and their services given to the State."[5] Had Louis and his successors paid as much attention to their military engineer's conscience as to his military advice, subsequent French and European history might have taken different routes in their not distant future.*

53. *Errard de Bar-le-Duc, ideal cities*

But Vauban's career and reputation were dominated by more conventional Baroque concerns: fortification systems and new towns which combined defense with necessary urban facilities. Responding to the increased power of contemporary artillery, he moved the lines of the ramparts farther out from the more contained fortified boundaries of earlier theorists and engineers so that a city's surrounding landscape was increasingly

* Not only was Vauban's advice ignored, but its implied criticism of national tax policies estranged him from the king and he died in disgrace.

consumed within the vast stellar sprawl of the outworks. These systems dwarfed the inner walls and bastions; some dwarfed even the city they were marshaled to defend. The city within its walls was left untouched in those cases where Vauban was charged with modernizing its fortifications (fig. 54). But when the planning of new towns was involved, the polygonal layout almost invariably enclosed a plan based on orthogonal principles. Charleroi was an exception to this standard, but it was early in his career (1666). His later, more ambitious and characteristic projects (Longwy and Saarlouis, 1679, and Neuf Bri-

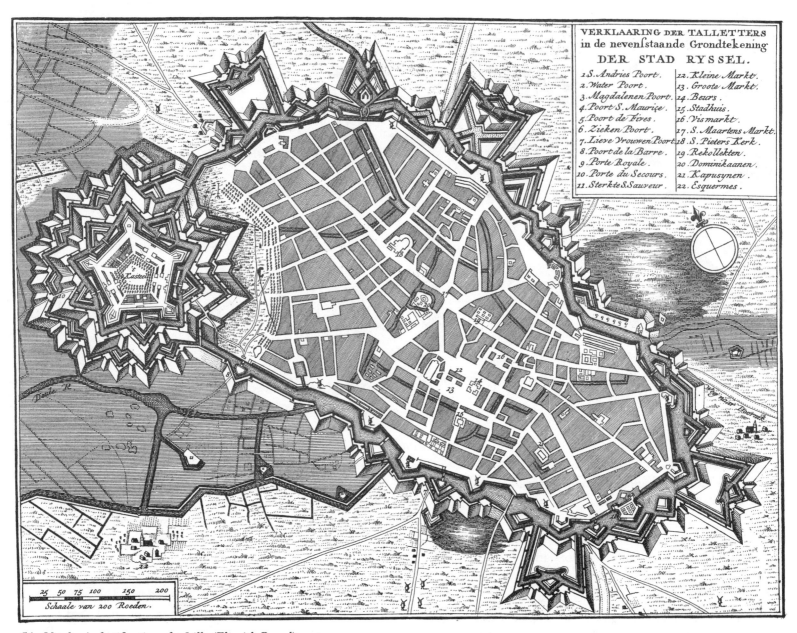

VERKLAARING DER TALLETTERS
in de nevenſtaande Grondtekening
DER STAD RYSSEL.

1. S.Andries Poort.   12. Kleine Markt.
2. Water Poort.   13. Groote Markt.
3. Magdalenen Poort.   14. Beurs.
4. Poort S.Maurice.   15. Stadhuis.
5. Poort de Fives.   16. Vismarkt.
6. Zieken Poort.   17. S.Maartens Markt.
7. Lieve Vrouwen Poort.   18. S.Pieters Kerk.
8. Poort de la Barre.   19. Rekollekten.
9. Porte Royale.   20. Dominikaanen.
10. Porte du Secours.   21. Kapusynen.
11. Sterkte S.Sauveur.   22. Esquermes.

25 50 75 100   150   200

Schaale van 200 Roeden.

54. Vauban's fortifications for Lille (Flemish Ryssel)

sach, 1698) were also representative of his preferred practice: each with polygonal city walls around a core of strictly grid-patterned streets and blocks. The emergency dash from the center to the bastions by radial routes was no longer a design factor; the distant line of lunettes was now the front line of defense, leaving the bastions and their support to less immediate roles. The city itself could thus be designed with more attention to conveniences and practicalities which the grid plan tended to offer. So his approach to the planning of circular cities relegated their people to the unrelieved uniformity of a rigid "science" that in plan at least suggested little of his professed sympathy for "les pauvres gens."

Not until the end of the eighteenth century does one begin to discover ideal city concepts that substantially manage this more generous dimension. Pierre Patte (1723–1814) was one such theorist. In his *Mémoires sur les objets les plus importans de l'architecture* (1769) he took note of urban needs beyond those of the aristocrats, decrying current preoccupations with monumentality and grandeur and the neglect of provisions for the general welfare—health, safety, sun, and air. Although he cautioned of the need for careful site selection (preferring the presence of a large east-west flowing river or two joining navigable rivers), he maintained a traditional loyalty to hexagonal or octagonal outlines where the topography would permit it. His rationale was that this made for a more cohesive city fabric and avoided the complications of too much distance within the city. "It is advisable, above all, to avoid monotony and unrelieved uniformity in the arrangement of its plan but, on the contrary, to aim for variety and contrast in the forms so that all the various quarters will not resemble each other."[6] Further advice had to do with the impact of climate on street design and building height, the threat to health posed by the practice of building houses on the city's bridges, and the design of streets in general for their safety and convenience.

A contemporary of Patte's, Claude-Nicolas Ledoux (1736–1806), was a similar transitional figure but one who, retaining a traditional plan approach, nevertheless brought a new liberating interpretation. In contrast to the long history of both Renaissance and Baroque ideal circular cities with their dense cores of development and rigid separation from nature, Ledoux's concept not only sought to achieve a new harmony between these two environments but even managed to demonstrate such a marriage in the design and partial construction of an ideal city. His *ville idéale* of Chaux (c. 1775, in northeastern France) placed its emphasis not on a palace but on the industry for which it was founded, a saltworks. The eighteenth century thus closed with the recognition of a new reality in society: the Industrial Revolution and the need for creating environments designed to house the processes and workers of a new era. Though Ledoux drew again on the circle, he offered it in ways that opened his city to the amenities of nature, weaving them into the fabric of his plan and the plan into the context of its area, rather than employing the form ritualistically as it had been in the past. Incorporating in his ideal city the presence and benefits of the natural world, Ledoux anticipated the Garden City a hundred years before that concept would become a familiar one in the planning vocabulary of the industrial city. In Ledoux the eighteenth century, at first preoccupied with the theatricalities and excesses of the Baroque city, began to make the philosophical and experimental transition to the urban realities and requirements of a new century.[7]

But there were also signs of change from other directions. The symbolic perfection of the circle, which through the centuries had built up such a universal literature and mystique, began in the eighteenth century to be called into doubt. Was the perfect order of the universe quite what it seemed, a system without blemish, based on the flawless beauty of the cir-

55. *An eighteenth-century English romantic landscape* (Dell' arte dei giardini inglesi, *1800*)

cle? Eighteenth-century science was contributing to these uncertainties; the irregularities of the natural world were more consciously perceived. The earth itself was now being recognized for what it was: no perfect sphere but encrusted with abrupt breaks in the thrust upward of mountain ranges and in the downward depths of the oceans.[8]

In fact, a new esthetic was emerging which denied that beauty was the derivative of an ordered hierarchy of geometrical shapes with the circle as its crown. From such rigid formulas some philosophers, artists, and other eighteenth-century intelligentsia were seeking relief in the unexpected pleasures and beauty of irregularity. This romantic sensibility, so well expressed and encouraged in the writing of Rousseau, sought to expand human appreciation of the natural world with its irregularities, its undulations, its rough and smooth contrasts, its spontaneity, and its subtleties—in sharp contrast to the balanced and honed formal mystique that had been institutionalized by Renaissance and Baroque philosophy, art, and society. The eighteenth-century English revolution in the art of the landscape and its Continental applications (fig. 55); the cult of the "natural man"; the enthusiasm for rococo decorative arts; the fashionable eccentricities of *sharawadji* (a taste for the inspiration and products of the Far East and for "careless or unorderly grace"): all were aspects of a weariness with the heavy hand of formal controls and formulas, whether in the social order or environmental arts. Yet, in spite of this late eighteenth-century ferment, the formalisms of cities in the round would continue to be applied intermittently.

Baroque Circular City Applications

It is a curious anomaly that the Baroque era, whose cities were to express the supreme extravagances of military preoccupations and secular drama and display, should have as its first urban example a planned circular city whose form was motivated by quite different concerns. But then this will be a reminder that Baroque enthusiasm in the arts was rooted in Counter Reformation policy and service to the Church, even though its ultimate employment would be by more worldly forces. The early seventeenth-century founding of Scherpenheuvel (Montaigu) in the then Spanish Netherlands recalls an earlier motivation for the design of idealized cities. The site from medieval times had been a much venerated spot, a hilltop on which grew a cross-shaped oak tree. Further enhanced among pious people by someone's placing of a statue of the

Virgin in its branches, its sacred reputation was secured in an incident of about 1514 involving, according to legend, the paralysis of a shepherd when he attempted to remove the statue from the tree. Thereafter famous as a pilgrimage center, it required permanent facilities. An early wooden chapel was shortly replaced by one of stone, and finally the governor, Archduke Albert, and his wife Isabella in 1606 decreed the building of a town as adjunct to the church.* The town's designer, Wenceslas Coeberger, an architect and painter, drew from Italian Renaissance ideal city sources, tempering his interpretation by reference to the symbolic significance of the number seven (and also coincidentally recalling the employment of the same number by the Dutch of the seven united provinces in their cities of Willemstad and Coevorden). For Scherpenheuvel, the seven radials of the sanctuary's park plantings and the city's seven-sided plan were chosen to symbolize the seven joys and sorrows of the Virgin (fig. 56). The east-west orientation of the city's main axis also linked the plan to Church cosmology. When at a later date (1630) fortifications were added at the request of the government, their design was of necessity determined by the previously-established religious rationale, which, however, was easily transposed to fit the technology of military science.[9] The city's plan centered about the seven-sided church, a reminder of the position Vitruvius had recommended for the "temple" but which it seldom earned in Renaissance or Baroque practice.

Today's Scherpenheuvel is still a national pilgrimage destination focused on the grounds of the shrine and the stolid domed presence of the church of Our Lady of the Oak Tree.

---

* Their action was not entirely due to spiritual motivations. The governor saw his encouragement of the shrine as a means for discouraging the inroads of Dutch Protestantism from the north.

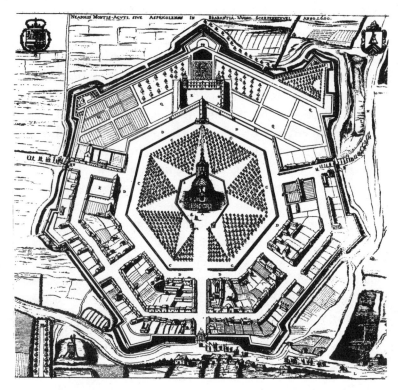

56. *Plan of Scherpenheuvel, 1660 (engraving by Q. Boel)*

by its founder, the Duc de Sully, for his fellow Protestants, and substantially followed the radial precedent of Villefranche-sur-Meuse, though considerably later (1608). One finds the same rigid square enclosure of the walls, which in this case embraces not a single radial pattern emanating out from the center but a further subdivision of the square into four quadrants, each with its own radial street divisions (fig. 57). The ideal cities of Perret or Salomon de Brosse (French architect, c. 1562-1626) with their radials and concentric squares could have influenced Henrichemont's design. The plan went beyond drier Renaissance ideal city interpretations but not so far

The sectors of the city plan east of the church remain open as an extension of the shrine's park (and as assigned by the original plan), but the remaining sectors of the heptagon are densely filled with commercial and residential development and temporary souvenir kiosks. So also are the frontages on those streets leading from the countryside into the original core. The walls no longer exist; they were removed in 1782.

Although Henrichemont, south of Paris, was not a planned circular city, its place in the sequence of events leading to such cities in France deserves mention here. It was designed

57. *Plan of Henrichemont, 1608*

as to depart from French loyalty to a bastide perimeter. It still reads clearly in today's quiet country town, much of which retains open space for gardens and orchards.

Charleroi of 1666, the work of Vauban, broke out of the bastide enclosure. It was one of his early new-city projects in a short string of radially-inspired strong points along the northern French border (from north to south: Charleroi, Philippeville, Marienbourg, and Rocroi). The city's plan retained the precedent of its neighbors' older plans, but fully developed a hexagonal outline with an elaborate system of fortifications typical of what would become standard in Vauban's military engineering practice (fig. 58). But henceforth the French, though now fully indulging in planned circular city designs, abandoned the radial aspects of ideal city theory. Their preference was for the pragmatics of grid plans. Changes also were being introduced in defense logistics, in large part resulting from Vauban's own elaborations of fortification science. Both contributed to the selectivity with which the French would apply theory to practice.

After Charleroi, Vauban's typical projects that set the military planning standards for decades were rigidly-organized grid plans contained within polygons of luxuriantly elaborate fortifications. Longwy of 1679 is representative (fig. 59). It embraced a system of large rectangular blocks about an enormous central square whose scale managed to obscure the presence of the substantial church which faced it. (A modern major street today slices through the city and expands the square's dimension well beyond Vauban's original generous dimensions.) A somewhat irregular site imposed itself on the hexagon of fortifications, which at one time entirely enclosed the city, built as part of Louis' defense system along the French-German border. But large portions of its walls to the north and west have disappeared to accommodate recent city growth, including a considerable hornwork which extended out to the northeast beyond the ditch. Longwy's modern center of gravity has shifted

58. *Plan of Charleroi*

from the heights of the original city into the valley of the Chiers River, which it had been built to dominate. Now a scruffy city, it is irregularly planned to fit the peculiarities of its site, plagued by a mountainous slag heap and brilliant orange clouds of industrial fumes.

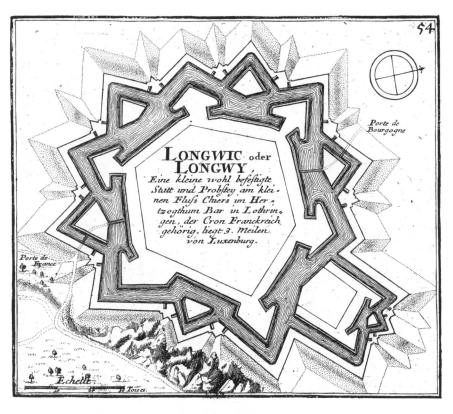

In the image: LONGWIC oder LONGWY, Eine kleine wohl befestigte Statt und Probstey am kleinen Fluß Chiers im Hertzogthum Bar in Lothringen, der Cron Franckreich gehörig, liegt 3. Meilen von Luxenburg.

Porte de Bourgogne

Porte de France

Echelle — Toises.

59. *Plan of Vauban's Longwy fortifications*

Both Saarlouis of 1679 and Neuf Brisach of 1698 in the perfect symmetry of their plans achieve unity between Italian-inspired ideal city concepts and Vauban's military and engineering science. Saarlouis, like Longwy, was designed as a hexagon, entirely symmetrical along its principal axis, including its hornwork extension across the Saar River (fig. 60). But for an almost totally preserved example of Vauban's military science and planning art brought to their most complete and highest level of development, one turns to Neuf Brisach on the Rhine River.

By terms of the Treaty of Ryswick of 1697, France had ceded the old city and fortress of Brisach to the Germans. But Louis XIV, recognizing the role that this area played as a route to Alsace, could not leave it a vacuum in his eastern defenses. Vauban was ordered to the scene and, after a number of alternatives were considered, recommended a site for new fortifications some distance to the west of Brisach. Not only did the location serve strategic purposes, but land, labor, and materials were all conveniently at hand for carrying out the project. Louis gave his assent, contractors were chosen, a chief of works, Jean-Baptiste de Regemorte, of Dutch ancestry and capable reputation selected, workmen from Brittany and Limousin brought in, and the work began.

Except for the Baroque splendors of Vauban's design for its defensive perimeter, much of the circumstances surrounding Neuf Brisach's planning and subsequent proselytizing closely followed medieval French bastide traditions. The plan was rigorously symmetrical and orthogonal (fig. 61). A generous Place d'Arme occupied the center, around which forty-eight blocks were ordered. Those facing the square, Vauban assigned to special purposes: the church, governor's palace, city hall, market hall, and quarters for various other high officials (only the church and palace ended up in the locations determined for them). The rest of the blocks were for the resident population. Ordinarily there would be ten houses per block for a projected total population of 3,500. In addition, barracks were to be built, two to house the infantry, two for the cavalry, 4,000 men in all. Vauban suggested several names for the new city: Brisac-le-François, Brisac-le-Roi, and Louis-Brisac. Louis preferred the name which after the Restoration assumed today's spelling: Neuf Brisach.[10]

60. *Plan of Saarlouis, 1713*

B.
des
Dames

Bastion de
la Saare

B. d'Einktrof

d'Allemagne

Fontaine

Batarde

B. de Liektrof

Bastion
de
Vaudrevange

Porte de France

Bastion
des
Bois

Saare R.

Prerie

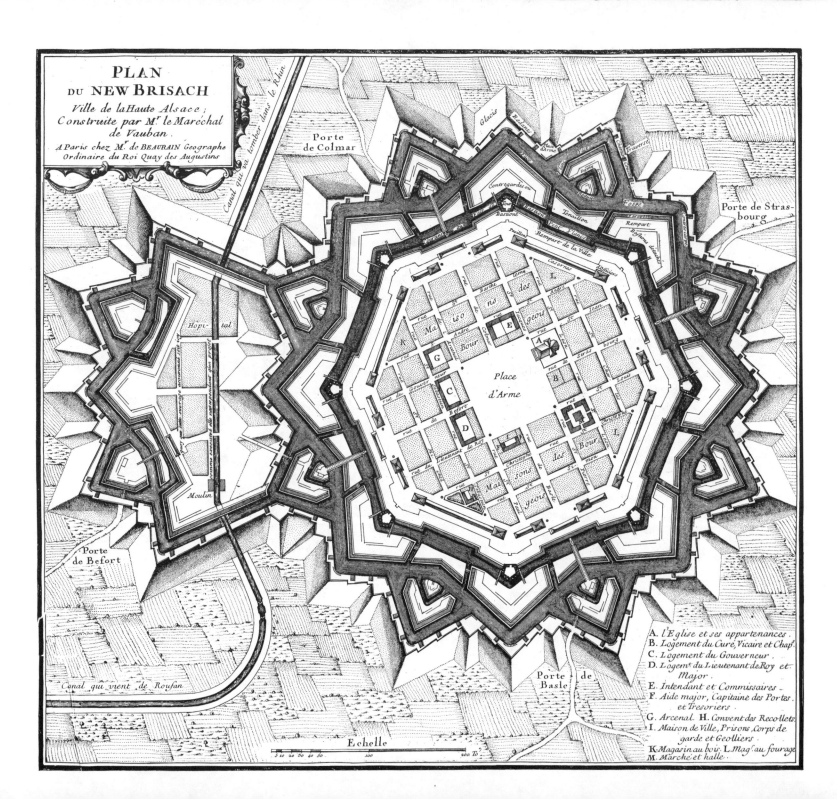

PLAN
DU NEW BRISACH

Ville de la Haute Alsace;
Construite par Mr. le Maréchal
de Vauban.

A Paris chez Mr. de BEAURAIN Geographe
Ordinaire du Roi Quay des Augustins

Porte de Colmar

Porte de Strasbourg

Porte de Strasbourg

Canal qui va tomber dans le Rhin

Hopital

Moulin

Porte de Befort

Canal qui vient de Roufan

Place d'Arme

Porte de Basle

A. l'Eglise et ses appartenances.
B. Logement du Curé, Vicaire et Chap.
C. Logement du Gouverneur.
D. Logemt. du Lieutenant de Roy et Major.
E. Intendant et Commissaires.
F. Aide major, Capitaine des Portes et Tresoriers.
G. Arcenal. H. Convent des Recollets
I. Maison de Ville, Prisons, Corps de garde et Geolliers
K. Magasin au bois. L. Magl. au fourage.
M. Marché et halle.

Echelle
5 10 20 30 40 50   100   200 To.

Also reminiscent of the bastides were the devices for encouraging settlement. By Louis' royal decree, special privileges came to the city and to those who took up residence in it. Land was free, though acceptance carried with it responsibilities for building there within two years, and only substantial construction of solid masonry stone or brick was permitted. The city was granted the right to hold fairs several times during the year, to have two market days a week, and trading rights free of local tolls and taxes. Nor could soldiers be quartered in the houses of its people.

Work proceeded quickly enough that by March 1702 the site was considered to be in a state of defensive readiness. The following year there were 1,500 inhabitants, and Neuf Brisach's future looked assured. But this was not to be. First came an outbreak of the plague, explained by contemporary observers as the consequence of foul airs released from the soils disturbed during construction. Vitruvius as a classical Roman had harbored the same misconceptions as to the role of the winds in disease transmission. Unhappily, Neuf Brisach would be beset by intermittent epidemics that discouraged its pace of development.

In addition, in September 1703, the French retook old Brisach.* Suddenly, the entire rationale for Neuf Brisach's existence was stripped away. Orders were issued to finish only that work already in progress; remaining funds were transferred to refortify old Brisach. It was at this time that Vauban's great hornwork was abandoned, together with its mill and military hospital. For eleven years Neuf Brisach was to linger in limbo.

Louis' further adventures and his signing of the Treaty of Rastadt in 1714 led to Neuf Brisach's reprieve. By the treaty's

* Vauban was one of the expedition's commanders. He had just been named a marshal of France.

61. *Plan of Neuf Brisach, c. 1710*

terms, old Brisach was lost a second time to the Germans, restoring Neuf Brisach's fortunes and permitting it over subsequent years to slowly follow the route of development leading to what we know today.[11]

As the result of its Rhineland location near the German border, Neuf Brisach was to undergo a history of vicissitudes, suffering especially as the consequence of the wars with Germany in 1870, 1914–18, and 1939–45. Incorporated into the Maginot Line defense system after the First World War, the city was occupied by the Germans from 1940 until liberation in 1945. Ironically, the destruction this time was at the hands of the Allies: American aerial bombing and artillery fire in January 1945 in the line of their advance. Reconstruction has now returned the city to a semblance of its traditional appearance (fig. 62). The ramparts, however, are the most historically authentic evidence of Neuf Brisach's past, a realization of Vauban's ideas at their highest level of development. Because of the unique status of these ramparts, the French government extended protection to them as a national historic monument (though not until 1970 when considerable deterioration had already taken place).[12] Conservation and restoration will thus preserve France's most substantial evidence of ideal city theory, harnessed though it was to the military necessities of her history.

Though political and economic circumstances in seventeenth- and eighteenth-century Italy made difficult the construction there of new cities in the ideal city idiom, it was not impossible. In fact, the only three such Italian cities sharing that idiom (two of which are in the round) are all in a most unlikely location: Sicily. That they should have appeared in what has traditionally been one of Italy's poorest, most backward, and misgoverned regions is testimony to the arrogance

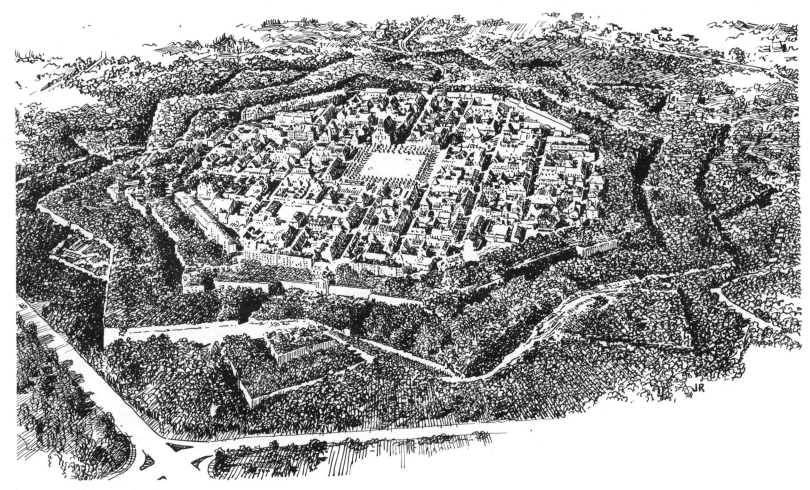

62. *Neuf Brisach* (Rohrer)

and obtuseness of the Baroque autocrats who sponsored them.

Sicily in the seventeenth century was nominally under the rule of the Spanish Hapsburgs, but the indifference of these colonial officials had come to mean in practice that control was largely in the hands of a few members of the local nobility and ecclesiastics. These formed a small but powerful elite, overweening in its ambitions and in its drive for recognition and prestige, whose vast holdings even included the peasants, disposable like the land they worked. This was especially true in the eastern half of the island where the absence of any middle class—independent farmers, merchants, or industrialists—permitted the rise of a feudal oligarchy of barons whose power was based on their absolute control over land, the economy, and political processes. (The latter included even the administration of criminal justice, purchased from King Philip III in 1621.) Another prerogative acquired by the barons from the king was the authority to extend land holdings into undeveloped areas and to populate them. As Maria Guiffrè notes, this was ostensibly for "the advantage that comes to the realm and *to those involved in rule* [emphasis added] and the fact that supplies of grain and other foods are increased, thoroughfare is assured for travelers, and payment of royal tribute in increased."[13]

This "advantage" not only was an aggrandizement of feudal holdings, but brought the barons directly into the process of land colonization. A consequence, especially during the seventeenth century, was the building of numerous small towns centering about feudal residences, an arrangement that demonstrated the barons' authority over the people in a manner reminiscent of imperial Chinese cities or Versailles. The hierarchical pattern of housing and its relationship to the baron thus reaffirmed in environmental terms the structure of the Baroque social order; these plantings were as much for satisfying personal drives and political ambitions as for meeting the needs of the people.[14]

Sixteenth-century ideal city theory had much appeal for the Sicilian aristocrats. In part this is a reflection of a culture lag between contemporary ideas on the mainland and those fashionable on an island separated both geographically and intellectually from current events. The work of Italian theorists and architects was stylish in Sicily at a time when it was already being overshadowed by other developments on the mainland. The isolated local aristocratic society warmed to a theory of abstract geometrical forms, an intellectualism that gave substance to an elitist need to appear erudite and *au courant*. The practicalities and realities of ordinary Sicilian existence were either ignored or sublimated in favor of ritualistic observances of theory—formal exhibitionism. Like their counterparts elsewhere,

Sicilian autocrats also saw the way the ideal city design vocabulary fitted exactly their own specifications for the environments they wanted to build and the relative positions which they and their peasants would occupy. The Renaissance circular city tradition thus was requisitioned in Sicily to serve an arrogant and outdated feudal society.

Sicily's three experiments in applied ideal city theory therefore emerged out of circumstances far removed from any ideal. Indeed, as if to remind one of the turbulence and tragedy of Sicilian history, two of the cities were born out of disasters: a landslide and an earthquake. Santo Stefano di Camastra resulted from the great landslide in 1682, which required the building of a new city. Located on the island's northern coast, its site is on a spur in rugged terrain overlooking the sea. The Duke of Camastra, fashionable in his familiarity with the ideal city literature, saw his new city as an opportunity for applying his learning to his own properties and proceeded to develop a noncircular plan with notable, if arbitrary, linkages to Renaissance theory. For the most part, his plan had streets oriented north and south, perhaps to receive the benefits of sea breezes (fig. 63). A grille was then superimposed over much of the pattern by a sequence of diagonals, resulting in an overall organization of streets and blocks remarkably similar to that of Henrichemont. The placement of the squares, however, varied from the latter. At Santo Stefano most were at the outer edges of the plan, facing the built-up wall of buildings which enclosed the city and together with the topography cut it off from the countryside. The city became a self-contained and artificial creation set down in its coastal landscape. The ducal palace opened to one of these squares to its south and to the north enjoyed vistas of the sea. The major church (one of six in the old city) faced the central square from which seven streets radiated. Most of the city was composed of the houses of its residents.[15]

In spite of a plan that appears to give priority to traffic and to make squares into traffic interchanges, the streets today manage the kind of liveliness characteristic of the Italian townscape. In addition, the design of the houses with external stairways helps to reinforce this communal interchange. Only the east-west main street connecting the two principal city gates discourages it. Environmentally, Santo Stefano is undistinguished; modern times have brought a southward sprawl whose monotony of long streets and rectangular blocks is more reminiscent of Manhattan Island than the Island of Sicily.

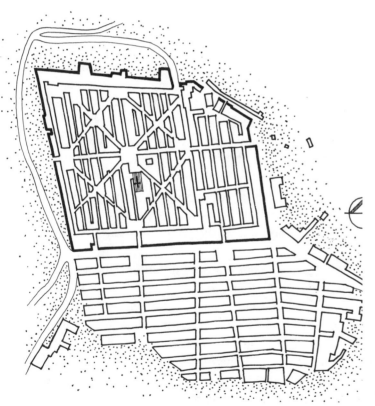

63. *Plan of Santo Stefano di Camastra with modern extensions*

The inspiration for Avola (fig. 64) could have been either Cataneo or Marchi, both of whom produced publications in the late Renaissance with diagrams that Avola's plan comes close to duplicating. Strictly a grid plan with a series of neighborhood squares at its perimeter, it was enclosed by typical Renaissance bastions and curtain walls in hexagonal form, protection that acknowledged its coastal location and potential for playing a defensive role. Avola's sponsors were two aristocrats, both "Marchesi di Avola," but the place of their actual residences within the town is not clear. There is a possibility they may have been located in the peripheral open space beyond the walls. Also elusive is any exact location for the original city hall. Only the church is clearly identified, on one of a series of small blocks that defined the outer edge of the town square. Perhaps it was built later, reducing in size what at one time would have been a square of considerably greater dimensions (rather on the scale of the Place d'Arme at Neuf Brisach).[16] There is no record of who was the city's actual designer, nor a clear-cut date for its founding, though the late seventeenth century is likely. By 1756 Avola was fully developed and compact within its walls. In a description of 1745, Avola was noted as being "surrounded everywhere by convenient courtyards meant more for protection in case of attack than for comfort which is provided by five large squares, some of which have a convenient public market where everybody may find what is needed."[17]

Today's Avola is almost entirely the product of the nineteenth and early twentieth centuries. Though the original city still reads in plan, its walls are gone. Sections of elongated rectangular blocks of modern development clumsily conflict with the inner hexagon of the old city. Both plan and architectural development have almost entirely obscured any sense of Avola's special place in Italian planning history.

With Grammichele, also conceived in disaster, we have

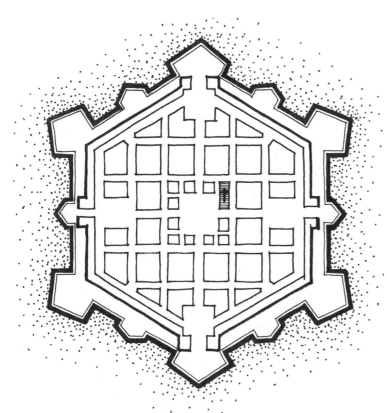

64. *Plan of Avola, 1756*

what must surely be one of the least known of the grand Baroque planning schemes for a new city. Even though Versailles and Karlsruhe outrank it, nevertheless Grammichele deserves to be included in that select group, in part because circumstances were so unlikely for it to appear at all. The city synthesized Baroque autocratic aspirations: it ignored the realities of a country and people, both plagued and impoverished by perennial misrule and injustice and just struggling out of the devastation of an earthquake. Their prince, not without some good intentions, chose an unusually extravagant plan for the new city. Rigid, ritualized, and dogmatic, its emphasis on

centrality is reflected in a geometrical and mechanical tour de force. Yet in spite of such artificialities, there is a certain bravado about the city's design and the audacity of the attempt that tends to deflect harsh judgments.

Grammichele rose out of the wreckage of the earthquake of 11 January 1693 in which the Noto Valley of eastern Sicily was ruined. Included in the total destruction was the small village of Occhiola on a site occupied since ancient times. Its feudal ruler, Carlo Maria Carafa Branciforte, prince of Butera and Boccella, moved quickly to reassure his peasants of the future by announcing the building of a new city for them—and him. The prince was a product of his times, though with certain more generous qualities that must have distinguished him from his contemporaries. He was an enlightened ruler, traveled and familiar with the culture of the mainland, well read, and a writer as well (he had a printing press brought to Sicily so he could publish his books). In addition—and this was most unusual—he had some social conscience. He wrote specifically of the prince's responsibility for listening to his people, visiting his properties to find out their needs for himself, and responding to them. Duties, not pleasures, must have first priority.[18]

The plan for his "new, very elegant town" (fig. 65) may well have been his own design with the assistance of a priest who was also an architect, Friar Michele dell Ferla. Both intellectuals, they drew from available sixteenth-century ideal city literature, perhaps modified by the example of Palmanova, which would by then have been well known. Both it and Grammichele were interpretations of plans radiating out from a central square with sectors clustered about a series of six neighborhood squares. The striking difference, of course, was the absence of any ramparts at Grammichele; the prince recognized that his city's remote inland location removed it from any serious threat of invasion, offering him the opportunity to avoid the enormous cost of ramparts. (Had they been a part of

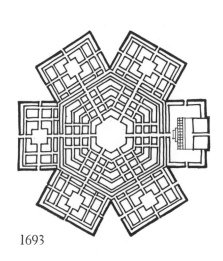

1693

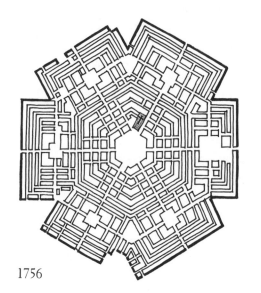

1756

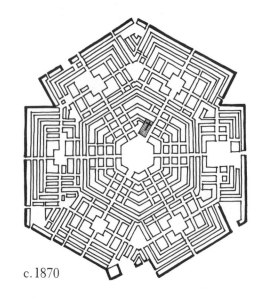

c.1870

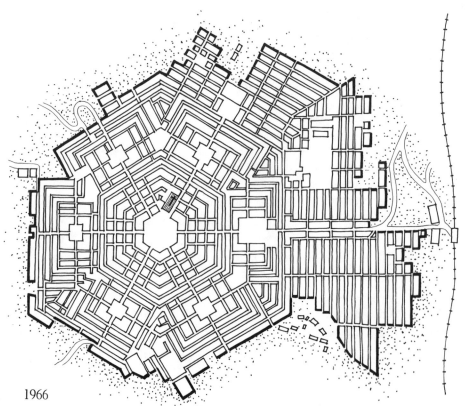

1966

65. *Grammichele's evolution*

the original construction, however, their presence would have subdued the pace of the plan's perimeter deterioration, which soon set in.) Perhaps the prince's enlightenment also took into account the nature of the city's population: most were peasant farmers, and the lack of ramparts made it possible for them to travel easily between the city and the land from which all drew their support. Once the city was planned, the prince moved quickly to bring it to reality by pledging money, offering building sites, and providing outside help for materials transportation and carpentry. He also promised rental concessions and various immunities and exemptions to encourage its populating. Some seven months after construction started, houses began to be occupied.[19]

Although Grammichele's plan had precedents in both theory and practice, its interpretation of them was highly individualized. Either the prince or his friar architect was unusually versatile in the handling of traditional themes. Six streets radiated out from the central square as at Palmanova, but from there on departures took over. Five of these radiating streets connected to outlying squares which acted as the central plazas for rectangular "borghi," or districts with their own internal grids. Between the borghi and the main square were fan-shaped sectors with circumferential and radiating secondary streets. The sixth radiating street led to the largest square of all and is believed to have been intended as the location for the residence of the prince (never built because of his early death). The outer triangular open spaces between the borghi were left open for close-in agricultural use. Development of the plan carried with it certain social implications. Housing on the major radial streets (and possibly surrounding the squares of the borghi) was reserved for the upper middle class. Their houses of two-story construction were built about an interior courtyard with workshops at ground level and housing above. But elsewhere one-story housing with small rooms, alcoves, and sheds was provided for lesser folk. Differentiation was further determined by varying lot sizes; these too reflected the social status of the future occupants.[20]

The principal public building was the main church, begun in 1724. Still the most prominent architectural monument of the city (rivaled in more recent years by the city hall across a side street), it displays none of the Baroque architectural flamboyance that was characteristic of the same period at Catania and would become that eastern Sicilian city's chief glory. The enclave for the unbuilt residence for the prince was given a privileged location by its axial connection with the most important of the routes leading into Grammichele, the road to Syracuse and the coast. The space remains partially unbuilt, the largest of the city's secondary squares.

Because no sharp line of defense locked it in place, Grammichele was to experience none of the static confinement of Palmanova or Neuf Brisach. Almost at once modifications took place in the development of the plan, which through the years evolved toward its present state. An early plan of the city as it initially developed shows certain variations already from that originally engraved by the friar architect, perhaps the result of unsophisticated builders inaccurately translating his plan. By about 1756 more changes had occurred, including a move outward of development lines with the borghi encroaching on their adjoining triangular open spaces. The ruling prince of the day published a ban that deplored the lack of order in this growth, complaining "that various usurpations had already taken place, that quite a few areas already assigned had not been built on, that several people owned building sites bigger than their needs, that a lot of other people were lacking basic necessities, and that several visitors had had to leave town because they couldn't find a decent place to stay. . . ."* New

*The latter condition still pertains today with the same consequences!

obligations were placed on owners to build within three years or release their property for others to do so.[21]

A process of accretion and encroachment continued through the eighteenth and nineteenth centuries. Development accelerated following the location in 1890 of the railroad station to the southeast, which gave special stimulus to movement in that direction. Subsequent years simply maintained the pace of this deterioration of Prince Carlo's great plan; only significant topographic breaks exerted any restraint over the city's development patterns. Now the skyline, which until recently had been largely uniform in height except for the profiles of the churches, is losing its continuity to modern construction and technology. Even with all its inflations and irresponsibilities, this splendid essay in Baroque planning still deserves better; but if the trend of its history is allowed to continue unchecked it may indeed have earned the fate of being forgotten.[22]

The grandiose formal potentials of ideal cities also had their attractions for the various Baroque monarchies of central and northern Europe. Karlsruhe was one of the most presumptuous, an enormous complex combining palace, garden, forest, and city into one coordinated and radioconcentric scheme which managed to imply that the whole universe was drawn into its web (fig. 66). A synthesis of the Baroque attitude, the whole composition radiated out from a central point, the palace of the prince. The local ruler, Karl Wilhelm, founded the city in 1715, originally as a hunting retreat, but in time he became more ambitious for it. Under him and successive rulers the palace was remodeled and extended, the gardens and forest were expanded, the radials (thirty-two of them projecting out from the palace tower) were laid down, and the city built with timbers was rebuilt in stone. A circular avenue defined the central area, but it marked no break in development; both city and forest extended beyond its limits, tied to the overall concept by the radials, which continued their sweep outward to the horizon, with no walls to impede these spatial dramatics.

Gutkind describes the city as

. . . a veritable pattern-book of ideas and prototypes ranging from the radial pattern of Palma Nova, the starlike design of new fortresses, and the diagonal streets of the Piazza del Popolo to the gardens of Versailles. It was a drawing-board plan, rigid, logical, and somewhat disingenuous, but it was a perfect symbol of the time, of the *l'état c'est moi* spirit of the absolute rulers.[23]

Karlsruhe suffered severely from the Second World War. The palace was entirely gutted, and destruction was general in the rest of the city. All that has now been repaired. Today the palace exterior has been restored to its original appearance; its interiors are deprived of their former rococo richness, but they have been splendidly converted to museum use. The rest of the city is also restored and thrives, sufficiently so to jeopardize its continuity with a past that in intent if not always in reality was the essence of Baroque theater, display, and extravagance.

The empire of the Hapsburgs was similarly inspired. When Nové Zámky was lost to the Turks in 1663, Leopoldov was built in Western Slovakia as a replacement. Its strictly radial plan and stellar ramparts show how much its builders had moved on from the Renaissance standards of Nové Zámky, adapting the ideal city format to the latest techniques of military science (fig. 67). Although Leopoldov remained a fortress city until its dismantling in 1854, it demonstrated that the circular city format and its refinements retained their place in the awareness of designers in the territories of the Austrian Hapsburgs.[24]

The Romanovs imported Baroque planning concepts to their

66. *Engraving of Karlsruhe, 1739*

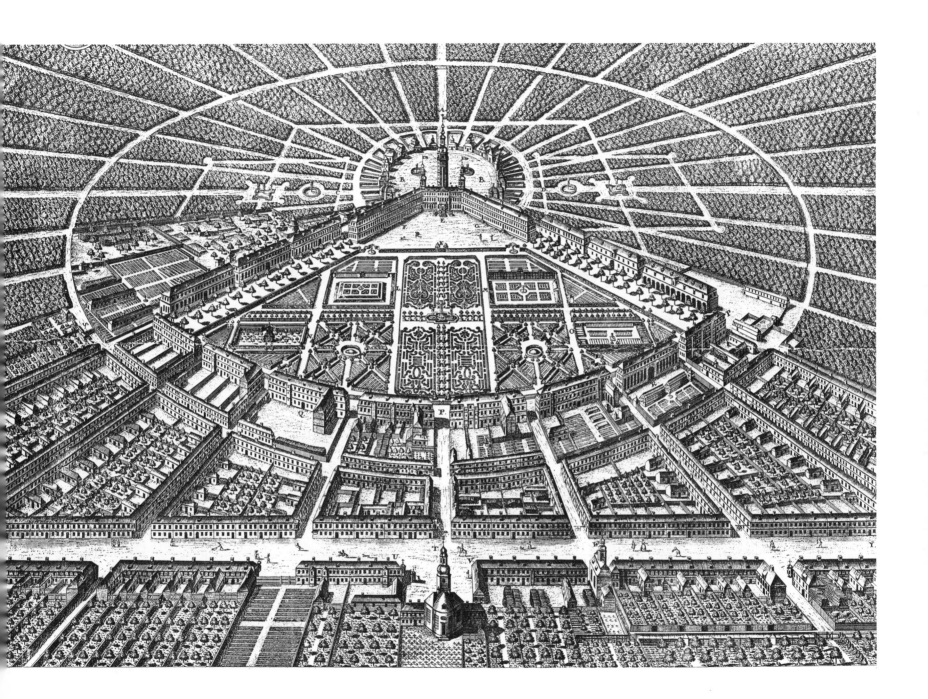

67. Plan of Leopoldov, seventeenth century

sprawling empire with more élan, but there is considerable doubt whether any local enthusiasm for ideal city theory had much to do with it. Rather, it seems more likely that Russia drew from sources already once removed, European cities and designers whose plans had already extracted and reinterpreted the formal language which was then further adapted for Russian usage. But whatever the circumstances, out of them was created a series of cities whose circular outlines and radial interior organizations came close enough to the others covered in this book to deserve their inclusion here.

Any conscious city planning came relatively late in Russian

history. The medieval forms of her cities and the spontaneous irregularity of walls and street patterns were compatible with the conditions of Russian life. The cities were themselves the instrument of governmental policy rather than products of the initiative of local burghers (there were none); their planting was for administrative or military purposes. In spite of this centralized sponsorship, there was no systematic approach to planning. The founding, design, and life of cities were clearly of low priority through the seventeenth century in Russia, cut off as she was from easy exchange with contemporary European events and planning practices. It was not until the reign of Peter the Great that significant new factors were introduced which by 1750 would redirect Russia's urban history. Peter, who was Czar from 1682 to 1725, was driven to wrench his country out of its Asiatic and medieval past and rebuild it, Westernized and modernized to match its potential for greatness in European affairs. His visit to Western Europe in 1697–98 had provided him with the standards to emulate in his own policy, and on his return to Russia he proceeded with ruthless dispatch to apply them. Russian city planning was a part of his focus. His activist foreign policy and his internal governmental reorganization stimulated the planting of new cities. Fortress cities were the result of the former; administrative capitals for regions, provinces, and counties were due to the latter. In addition, the gradual rise of a merchant class and aristocracy by the beginning of the eighteenth century began to lend support to city development, augmenting official efforts. The building trades were encouraged as well as local manufacturers, all contributing to a social foundation on which Russian urban workers' settlements began to appear, in addition to city types more directly the product of governmental policy.

This period also witnessed another change: planning based on policy and system where none had existed before. More permanent types of development were introduced: paved

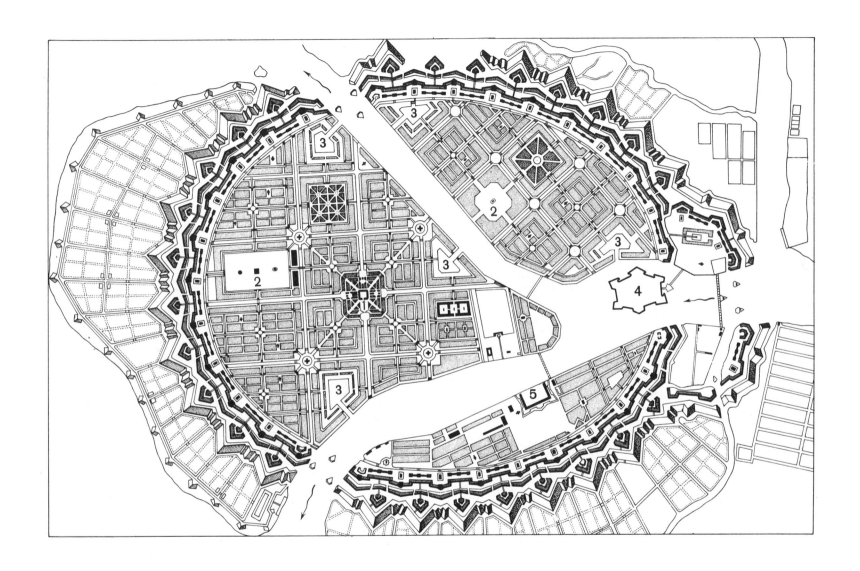

68. *Le Blond, plan for St. Petersburg, 1717*

streets, improved maintenance standards, drainage, lighting, and street trees. With the state as the principal client for the building of cities, administrative standards also appeared, including building commissions and code requirements for determining how cities were to be laid out, as well as how they would be built. It was a time when the old spontaneous patterns and practices gave way to regularization. No longer would the streets be "forced into narrow, crooked, and torturous shapes according to the individual owner's whim. . . ."[25] By 1750 Russia had completed this evolution, had founded a host of new towns, and was ready for the

grander Baroque forms already long fashionable in West European cities.[26]

When the time came, Russia had a more directly available example to examine, closer to home and heavy with prestige: her new capital city of St. Petersburg. This was the city that Peter had announced would be Russia's new capital, his window to the west. His goal was to create a city that in all ways would declare its rejection of medieval Moscow and display to the nation and the world Russia's assumption of membership in the modern community of European nations. For his chief architect and planner, Peter chose a Frenchman, Jean Baptiste

Holy Cross

Yelizavetgrad

69. Plans of late eighteenth-century Russian fortress cities

Alexandre Leblond (1679–1719), familiar with Paris, with Versailles, with Vauban's work, and with certain of the theorists such as Dilich—thoroughly grounded, therefore, in the standards of French Baroque planning which by then were the standards of Europe. Although the plan he prepared for St. Petersburg (fig. 68) was not to be realized, its design spirit and usages were to be influential as a model for the crop of new cities and revisions of the old that would appear in Russia in the last half of the century. Sibyl Moholy-Nagy notes that

Leblond's plan of 1710 [for St. Petersburg] underwent many modifications in its final form, but the original plan illustrates clearer than most other absolutistic schemes the cosmic-dynastic grand illusion. There is again the Assyrian inclusion of the river as chief artery and, in its natural frame, the great palace, sending its rays of surveillance and benevolence into the four corners of a geometrically-disciplined urban universe.[27]

Such a planning spirit complemented handsomely the Baroque autocracy of the czars. In fact, both St. Petersburg's unrealized plan, and the spatial drama of the city that was eventually to be, had far more impact on Russian planning practices than the inaccessible works of the theorists or those remote specialized cities they had influenced. This also may account for the fact that, though there were early eighteenth-century fortresses with full radial and circular stellar plans and one city of the same period with a partial plan,* no Russian city fully employed the prototype circular city plan.

*Holy Cross Fortress in the northern Caucasus and Yelizavetgrad in southern Russia (fig. 69). Gutkind provides a plan of the late seventeenth-century fortified city of Taganrog on the Sea of Azov which is shown with six of its ten radial sectors complete (fig. 70). The rest are sacrificed to rectangular fortifications that extend into the sea. (Gutkind, *Urban Development in Eastern Europe*, p. 298)

70. *Plan of Taganrog, late eighteenth century*

The last half of the eighteenth century saw an influx of rationalized and elaborate planning schemes into Russian practice, some of them distinctively circular and radial, though modified in form. The absolute authority of the czars was to be accurately mirrored by the arbitrary and capricious impositions of these schemes, even though as plans they are delights to the eye. Most of the new cities appeared on rivers, which typically were more reliable for both winter and summer travel than the road system. However, with the breakup of ice in the spring, bridges could be destroyed, an additional encouragement to confine more modest cities to one bank. As a result, the riverfront locations imposed more rigorous natural disciplines on the planner than did the smooth, uninterrupted, flat sites preferred in Western Europe. Such Russian locations also contributed to the neglect of the full ideal urban form (though there were instances in Western Europe where similar river sites had not denied the planning of a fully circular city, for example Saarlouis or the ideal river cities of Dilich).

Bogoroditsk of 1778 was typical of these partial applications.

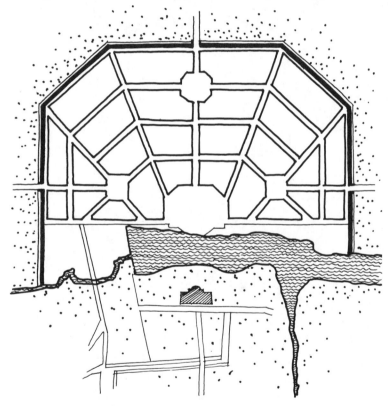

71. *Plan of Bogoroditsk, 1778*

Catherine the Great had chosen the former site of a seventeenth-century fortress for the building of a palace for herself south of Moscow overlooking the Ypert River. On the opposite bank west of her palace was laid out a polygonal planned city (fig. 71). The palace and its grounds were quite independent from the city except for an east-west axial relationship between the two, centering, of course, on Catherine's palace. The city's plan was based on a series of five radial streets, three of which sprang from the central plaza, open on one side to the river and duplicating the city's polygonal perimeter. The radials and four concentric streets connected riverfront to interior blocks. There were also three other lesser squares symmetrically placed within the overall scheme: one a marketplace, the other two for churches. Vlacheslav Shkvarikov describes in further detail the city's development, how it occurred bit by bit, the surveyors laying out the rays and setbacks with trees and turf placed on both sides of the streets. After the rays were established, the surveyors determined the concentric rings. Only then was construction started on one-story buildings along the setback lines.[28] Shkvarikov also shows plans of other Russian cities that were variations on circular city themes hinting at ideal city conceptual possibilities; none fully adopted them (fig. 72). All were provincial cities of various pretensions which hoped by following the fashions of the capital to enhance their own prestige, regardless of the appropriateness of the model to their needs.

West from Russia and sharing the Baltic Sea with it was the kingdom of Sweden, whose territories included Finland. The frictions between the two Baltic powers encouraged fortress design in the same way that they had along the French-German border, though here on a much reduced scale. Nonetheless, Sweden and Finland, though well removed from the centers of ideal city speculations and Renaissance planning ideas, were by the seventeenth century aware of both and had already built

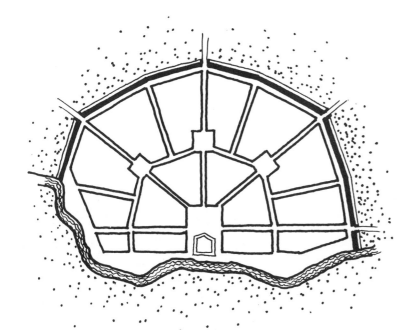

Luykh (1781)

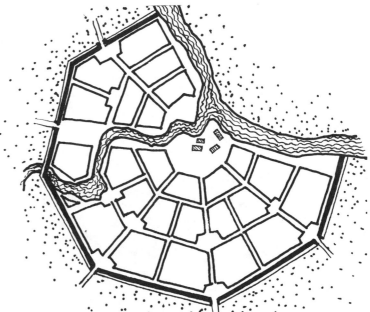

Lyuvim (1784)

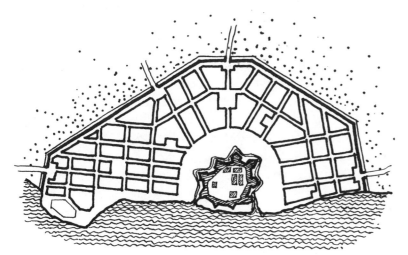

Rostov (1779)

72. *Various eighteenth-century Russian semicircular cities*

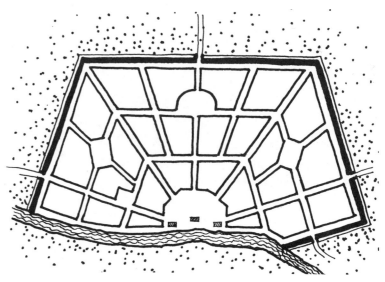

Glazov (1784)

73. *Plan of Hamina, c. 1750*

plied in the context of the circular city vocabulary, is found at Hamina.

Hamina did not start out with an ideal city plan but was one of those Finnish cities of the seventeenth century whose original design had routinely followed the orthogonal standards of the Renaissance. Located to be an intermediate port and urban center between Helsinki to the west and Viipuri to the east, it was laid out in 1649 by Erik Nilsson Aspergren as a series of north-south rectangular blocks to form a composite east-west rectangular plan without walls. An existing medieval church on the site was incorporated into the plan with its own off-center reserve. This new town of Weckelax Nystad was recognized by a charter of 1653. Subsequent growth was slow, amounting to hardly more than a few hundred persons when war and fire in 1712 destroyed the town. The rebuilding was also the occasion for replanning. But a new factor had been introduced: the city was to become a fortress, calling for an entirely different planning approach. The plan by Axel Löwen that followed in 1722 turned to the ideal city format, providing the concept with its most northerly application (fig. 73). The resulting city (renamed Friederichshamn for King Fredrick I), as it gradually developed, had much of the flavor of Palmanova, though adjusted to the more limited circumstances of Finland and the peculiarities of the site. This latter was a salt-water-bordered peninsula area, insufficient in breadth for the full sweep of the city's polygonal ramparts. In Löwen's original plan they were left open to the northeast, on the assumption that the bluff there and the water below would provide adequate protection. Later the fortifications were completed by flattening them out as an adjustment to this topography.

Work on these ramparts provided the city with a stellar arrangement of bastions and curtain walls, ditches, lunettes, and

74. *Hamina (Rohrer)*

something of a record in applying them to local needs. Although Finland has never been a country of many cities (some seventy-eight of them exist there today), fifteen were being planned or built during the seventeenth century, and the regularized grids of Renaissance inspiration were familiar to Finnish planners. The steady rhythm of straight streets and rectangular blocks relieved by the unpretentious presence of a Renaissance-style city square were comfortable practices. Pori, Oulu, Tornio, Helsinki, and Kajaani were among those cities whose plans established such methods in the Finnish experience.[29] But the most clearcut evidence of those practices, ap-

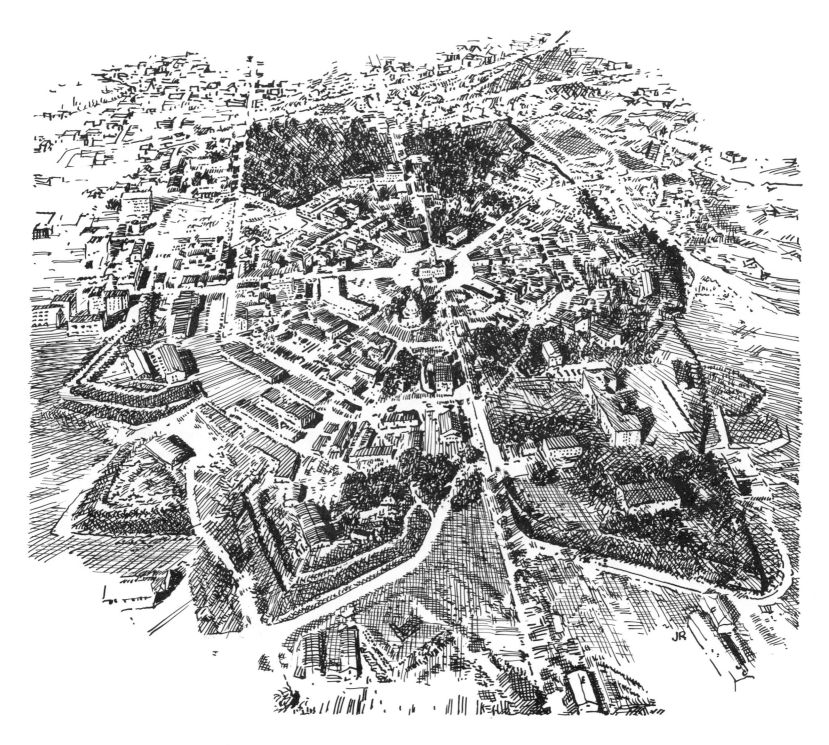

glacis in an impressive importation of Vauban's science. First the Swedes, then the Russians (who gained control of the city in 1743) continued with these works through the eighteenth and into the early nineteenth century. Within the ramparts' enclosure the 1722 plan maintained an entirely regularized octagon of building blocks radiating out from the central square and defined by eight radial and two circumferential streets. These were gradually built up mostly with private single-story wooden houses, which of course increased the city's vulnerability to fire (there were two severe fires in the first half of the nineteenth century). The original plan consigned no structure to the central square, but the city hall was built there in 1798. Subsequently, two of the inner blocks adjoining the square and opposite each other were given over for church purposes, one for the Lutheran Church (1843) and the other for the Russian Orthodox Church (1837).[30]

In the adjustments following the end of the First World War, the Republic of Finland was created, and Hamina (its commonly used and now official Finnish name) became a part of the new nation. No longer of any military significance, Hamina had in the late nineteenth century already broken through part of its walls to surround itself with a grid-planned fringe of streets and blocks which would accommodate future expansion. Today that expansion has to some extent been realized (fig. 74). However, the bulk of modern development has taken lines of less resistance with an irregularity of plan to match that of the shorelines and topography. Because of its role as a deepwater harbor and oil depot, Hamina has since the Second World War far outgrown the confines of its ideal city core, and although much of the old ramparts remains, their potential as an open space, recreational feature, and historic monument has only been partially realized. Nor has much of the modern construction in the inner city been responsive to the city's unique place in urban history. Some of

the streets, still lined with picturesque wooden single-story buildings, convey a considerable sense of the nineteenth-century Russian city, but this continuity has too often been broken by the disharmonies of new development. There is, however, local interest in recognizing and preserving Hamina's past. An official planning office operates there, studies have been completed, and some restoration work has been undertaken. If this continues, Hamina may be able to preserve the evidence of its unique past, and the historic fabric of this most northerly of the ideal cities could well have a future of some permanence.

If the eighteenth century seemed cut off entirely from the ties that held the circular city, however tenuously, to social concerns, the internal convulsions of that century were to bring such concerns back as a significant force in the shaping of its last ideal city, Chaux. By the date of Chaux's construction, about 1775, the American Revolution had begun and the French Revolution would soon be at hand; agitation had broadened sufficiently to require reconsideration of such questions as the needs and rights of the individual and of the broad masses of human society. Even in the late eighteenth century, attention was beginning to focus on the worker in an industrial city.

Chaux's designer, Claude Nicholas Ledoux, was a visionary architect who had already demonstrated the affinity he felt for the symbolic potential of circle, sphere, and square. Sometime around 1770, he had designed a cemetery in the form of an enormous sphere rising out of a square foundation structure, the mystic circle within the square. He had also planned caretaker residences as free-standing spheres, as well as other, more monumental buildings, all of which reaffirmed his attraction to circular and spherical forms. For the planning of Chaux

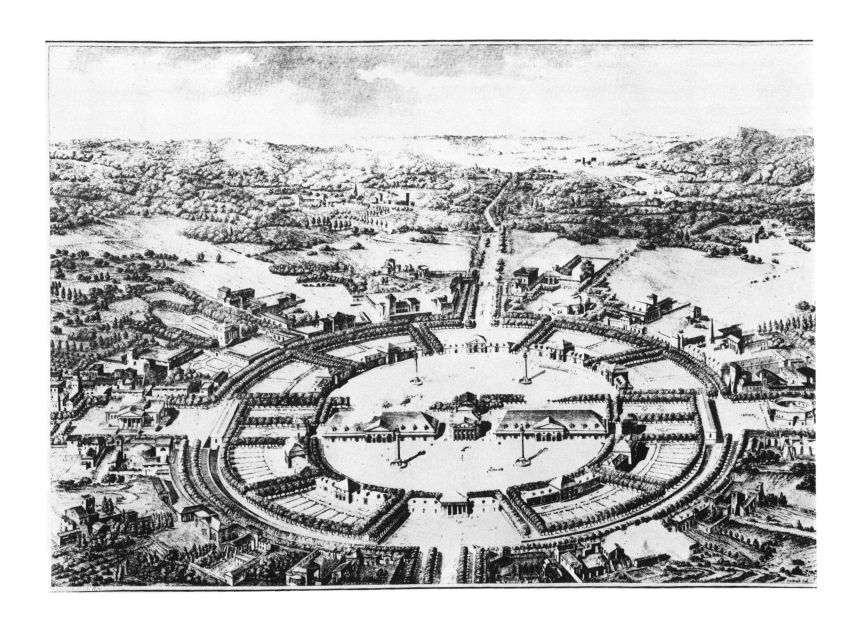

75. *View of Chaux*

(on a site north of Besançon in northeastern France), he designed facilities to house the processes and workers for the state-owned manufacture of salt. His first scheme was confined to that function, though on a grand scale. It was entirely square in outline with a monumental internal organization of spaces and functions in a totally symmetrical pattern. His authorization must have been broadened, for the plan he next prepared was for a complete city. Ledoux had set for himself the task of planning an ideal city that for the first time was to be an industrial city as well.

For the overall shape, he selected a great oval because of its "forme pure comme le soleil dans sa course"; it centered on the crossing of two major axes at right angles to each other (fig. 75). In the middle, along the short axis of the oval, were the director's house, administrative buildings, and the salt works, with city hall, courthouse, parsonage, and paths located in various other axial positions in the plan. Unusual attention was also given to the workers' housing; Ledoux was specifically (and unconventionally) concerned that their quality of life—their health and happiness—should be raised by his design. He provided for communal as well as private functions. Some of the facilities were shared service rooms, others private, including quarters for families; garden and orchard allotments were also provided. Instead of ramparts there was an outer line of gardens enclosed by a low elliptical wall and a greenbelt of trees paralleling the ring road. Beyond was the open countryside, making Chaux the first Garden City of an industrial community.[31] The architecture for all this, whatever the function, was consistently monumental, with great stone porticoes, arches, pediments, and hip roofs, rather authoritarian in its strength of form, symmetry, and originality of detail. But as a late eighteenth-century architect and theorist, Ledoux did much at Chaux to reaffirm, after long neglect, the commitment of the planned circular city to the search for environ-

ments designed to enhance life rather than to intimidate it.

Only half of Chaux was ever built (fig. 76), and it gradually deteriorated into private ownership and neglect. But in recent years it has been rescued from this fate, with the French government undertaking its restoration. It is now part museum, part European conference center for the contemplations of "futurologists"—meaningful modern roles that happily complement Ledoux, his vision, and the ideal city that he shaped.

The urban planners of the seventeenth and eighteenth centuries, dominated as they were by the autocratic institutions of Baroque life and the widespread preoccupation with nationalism and aggression, found in the circular tradition useful devices which could be manipulated to serve contemporary concerns. Though some of the literature of the time demonstrated an awareness of the theoretical traditions of ideal city thinking, except for Scherpenheuvel and Chaux the cities actually built were submerged in the physiology of defense and formal ritual. Their secularized realities bore witness to the extent to which the city in the round, while persisting, had been enslaved by a quite different set of masters and values.

The closing years of the eighteenth century in the West were dominated by the turmoil of revolution: philosophical, economic, and political. All of these challenged or overwhelmed the traditional order that had dictated human relationships, and challenged also the environmental forms that mirrored them. The nineteenth century was to have its own set of priorities and requirements which would seem to break permanently with all the traditions of the past. Yet the planned circular city, in spite of such unfavorable prospects, would continue to find a place in ideal city conjectures and the city-building practices of the new century and the one that was to follow.

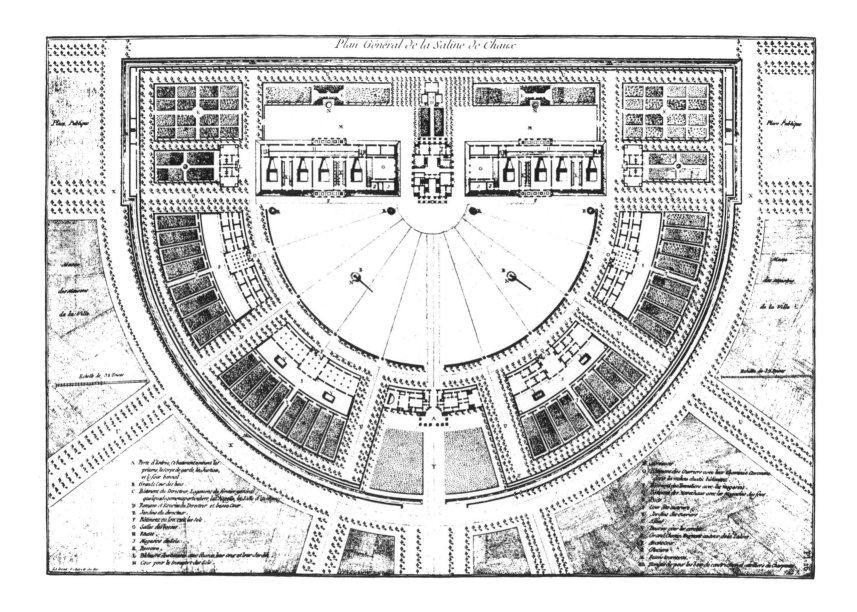

76. *Ledoux,* plan of Chaux

VII. Circular Cities of the Nineteenth and Twentieth Centuries

CITIES in the round continued to be built in the last two centuries, but on mostly new terms. Reflecting the changing priorities of the times, advocacy of a circular order was not for its cosmic implications or enhancement of religious authority, nor even for its military convenience. Instead, circularity would be embraced for its perceived secular virtues of egalitarianism and efficiency, "sanitary Utopias of Spartan simplicity,"[1] or as a means to success in speculative venture. The philosophical aspirations of the circular city might in some cases retain a certain sociological grandeur or remnants of cosmology. In other cases its traditional political linkages would linger in service to the vanity of a dictator or to visions of a capital for a twentieth-century developing nation. But the greater likelihood was that its use would be more pedestrian and contained: the housing of an agricultural or workers' colony, or merely an unconventional platting device drawn up by real estate promoters to entice purchase.

Modern Theorists

Étienne Cabet (1788–1856) is a figure who even in the nineteenth century maintained some continuity of the planned circular city with utopian ideals. Though he lived through France's revolutionary travail, his reformist enthusiasms earned him banishment to England where he spent his time in exile writing *Voyage en Icarie* (1840). In it he described an ideal communistic society in which the family was the only unit with any independence. All other aspects of life—economic and social—were controlled by a popularly-elected government whose authority was expressed through elected deputies. (Cabet had himself been such a deputy in the France of Louis Philippe.) In establishing the form of the capital of Icaria, Cabet turned once again to a planned circular city. Its outline was an almost perfect circle through which was directed a river whose Scamozzi-like alignment had been adjusted to conform to the city's orthogonal plan. At the city center the river separated to surround a circular island which was the landscaped setting for the principal public buildings and an open square. The square included a column and statue sufficiently "immense" and "colossal" to dominate the rest of the city. Alberti's domed central building would have done likewise. The balance of the city, rigorously symmetrical with straight streets and rectangular blocks, was filled with the houses and gardens of the capital's residents. Cleanliness, efficiency, convenience (including a public transportation system), and order were all high among Cabet's priorities; state planning was guided by the will of the nation and thereafter codified by laws prescribing the ways and means for life in Icaria (and proscribing any potential for the spontaneous and the unexpected).[2]

But most circular city literature of these times departed from traditional idealism, confining itself to more pragmatic or pedestrian expectations. Robert Pemberton's Happy Colony (1854) would have been such a place. England by the mid-nineteenth century had already realized most of the unhappier social and environmental consequences of industrialization, and these had encouraged at least a few people to search for environmental alternatives. A sprinkling of model villages in the Midlands, the efforts of Robert Owen at New Lanark, and Sir Titus Salt's Saltaire each recall such early efforts. Pemberton added to that record. His proposal called for migration from England's crowded conditions to the open space and cheap land of New Zealand. There he proposed the building of a community which combined communal ownership of land with a certain amount of social innovation (voluntary labor, and work assignments that emphasized versatility of activity rather than deadening specialization). The plan for the colony was circular and radial, rather like that of Chaux, which is considered to have been one of Pemberton's influences (fig. 77). But he also declared that "all the grand forms of nature are round," a bias he shared with the Renaissance. In his case this belief was more an unconscious rationalization of his preference for circular form than a result of any acute observations of nature.

This city of "Queen Victoria" was by his specifications "to be perfectly round, about a mile in diameter, and taking the form of belts or rings, which will become larger as they recede from the centre. The roads to be wide and spacious, and planted with ornamental trees, as shown in the pictorial plan, in which is also shown the manner of dividing the lands around the town."[3] At its center was a model farm in a circular open space enclosed by four curved buildings, designated as colleges, whose iron and glass structures recalled the contemporary enthusiasm for Paxton's Crystal Palace in London of 1851. Groups of monumentally-designed buildings with uniform height surrounded this civic center and lined the streets,

providing a regularized urbanity. A splended tree-lined esplanade followed the city's circular outline and separated it from the open lands beyond. Streets were circumferentially and radially organized out from the center, the radials reaching into the countryside with its symmetrical scattering of farmhouses and fields. Pemberton's expectation was that his colonization program would support 100,000 families in this combination of cosmic symbolism and nineteenth-century pragmatic idealism.[4] None of it, however, was ever to be built.

Surely the similarities between the plan Pemberton developed for his Happy Colony and Ebenezer Howard's Garden City are more than coincidental. Howard was an unlikely candidate for the special position he was to occupy in the search for an environment to match the needs and circumstances of an industrial society. He was a court reporter with none of the usual credentials of the environmental professional; but his observation of nineteenth-century urban conditions both in Great Britain and in the United States inspired him in his search for alternatives. Realistic about the amenities and failings of both town and country life, his theory was intended to build on their separate positive values and to avoid their negatives to achieve the best of both in "town-country"—the Garden City.

Although no mention is made of any dependence on Pemberton, Howard in his *Tomorrow: A Peaceful Path to Real Reform* (1898; reissued with slight revisions in 1902 as *Garden Cities of To-Morrow*) included the communal ownership of land, and diagrams of his proposed city followed along lines almost identical to those of Pemberton's Queen Victoria (fig. 78). At least up to the perimeter of their circles there was the same central open space (where Howard located a garden rather than a model farm), a ring of public buildings to form the space's enclosure, a grand avenue of landscaped circumferential open space, and a system of radial and circumferential streets, the former acting as linkages from the city to the open

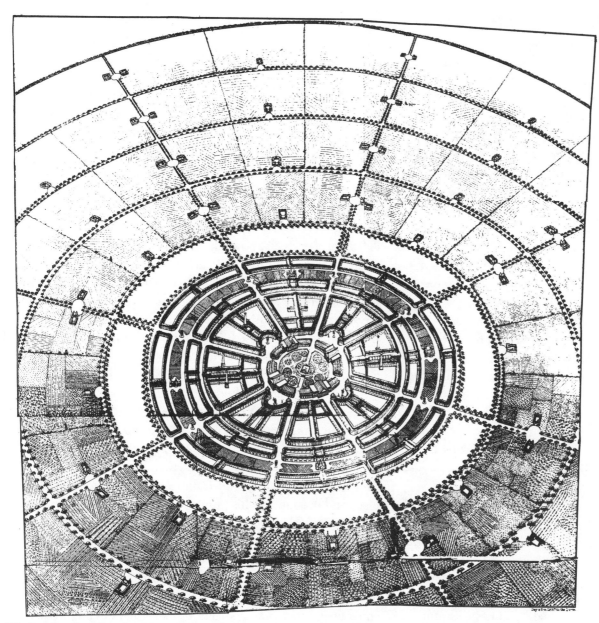

77. *Pemberton, plan for Queen Victoria town, 1854. Reprinted from Gutkind*, Urban Development in Western Europe: The Netherlands and Great Britain (*copyright © 1971 by The Free Press, a division of Macmillan Publishing Co., Inc.*)

lands beyond. Howard's delimitation between urban and agricultural land was sharper, the importance of the "Circle Railroad" gave his city a late nineteenth-century flavor, and his architectural specifications were open-ended in contrast to Pemberton's; but the essential lineage nevertheless is clear. However, whereas Howard participates in the long history of circularly conceived ideal cities, he does so in one markedly different way: his circular plans were intended to be no more than diagrams, clearly labeled as such. They were meant only to show a generalized context and relationship.[5] Indeed, the two cities most directly the result of his guidance (Letchworth of 1903 and Welwyn Garden City of 1920—both English) give no hint of the circularity of the theory that inspired them. (Nor did any of those that continued in the Garden City tradi-

tion in the active new-town construction program in Britain following the Second World War.) Only in his diagram did Howard add to the record of the planned circular city as a means for achieving improved lives for workers and their families in an industrialized world—with one fleeting exception. This was a community experiment in California, but, as will be explained, it never managed more than a momentary presence and then only as plan.

Twentieth-century urban theory was not, however, to be entirely removed from concepts having ties with cosmic city traditions or from Howard. Both these associations are found in the investigations of two German theorists of the early part of the century. Ernst Gloeden in 1923 offered a refinement of the Garden City in a proposal for an association of interrelated

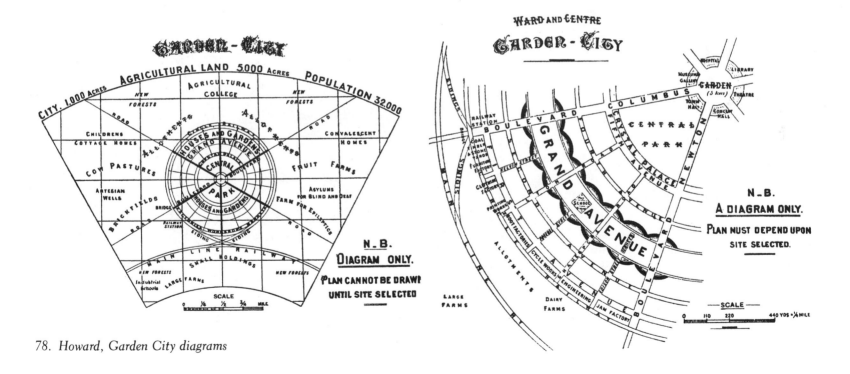

78. *Howard, Garden City diagrams*

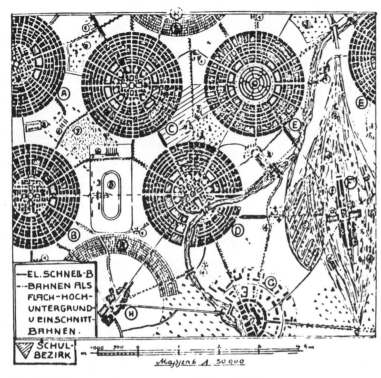

79. Gloeden, *circular cities regional plan, 1923*

the urban core or easily accessible to it. In his drawings, space becomes the binding agent of the city, whose structure is made visible and perceptible by the clarity and consistency of its circular and radial plan. These units would be satellite to existing concentrations and, as with Howard, become a means for their decentralization. Wolf's schematic city (dated 1919) has all the purity and uncompromising self-confidence of its Renaissance antecedents.[6]

There is one other theorist whose thoughts about our urban future have led him into unique cosmic city variations, the "arcologist" Paolo Soleri. Rejecting the horizontal generosity of Garden City derivatives, Solari would have us initiate the pro-

circular urban units (figs. 79, 80). Each of these units would combine housing and working areas within a fifteen-minute walking distance of each other. The units would in turn have easy access to open land and recreational space and be joined by a transportation web into a larger urban context.

A contemporary, the architect and planner Paul Wolf, followed theoretical lines that led him in directions closer to Howard. Wolf picked up the Garden City theme but treated it in ways openly returning to the circular city (fig. 81). Like Howard, he was attempting to use open space to break down the city's isolation from its amenities so that forests, fields, parks, playgrounds, and gardens would be woven directly into

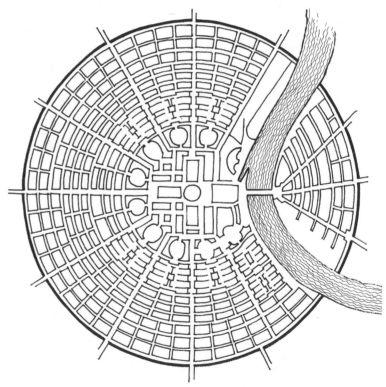

80. Gloeden, *plan of a circular city, 1923*

cess of "miniaturization" by the conscious employment of forms and technology to create cities of intense density (fig. 82). His arcology is a union of architecture and technology meant to substitute other amenities for that of infinite urban development in an all too finite world. Not expansion but compaction is his answer: urban organisms that build up and burrow down with structures of enormous plan and sectional intricacy and elegance, some versions of which borrow again from the efficiencies of the circular plan. His formal rationale has a certain familiarity:

Structural symmetry is probably observed throughout the universe. It is the necessary balancing of stresses that finds its patterns around points, lines, planes, and spaces of symmetry.
. . . Formal symmetry might well be the imprint of all other kinds of symmetry into the mind and the sensitivity of man. Even if the impositions of structure and function were lifted, impositions that result in formal symmetry, there would still linger in man the need for visual and in general sensorial symmetry. . . . It is to be noted that arcology is never symmetrical for the individual user. In other words, the individual user is always eccentric to the whole: symmetry in the whole, singularity in the parts.[7]

Earlier cosmic cities sought to build on foundations that were divine: forms and patterns that drew inspiration from celestial systems and order. Soleri's vision is convoluted and pessimistic; his modern city is a crushing creature of technology, remote in both time and spirit from the spaciousness of its ancient origins.

Apart from Soleri, most modern theorists, including those whose influence has been most effective or whose insights more accurately anticipated the inevitability of contemporary urban processes, have neglected the circular city in their repertoires. Both LeCorbusier's Ville Radieuse and Frank Lloyd Wright's Broadacre City conformed consistently to orthogonal planning approaches. But the circular city plan has neverthe-

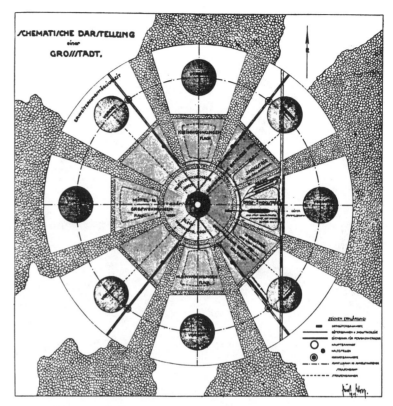

81. Wolf, diagram for a circular city, 1919

less had an intermittent but interesting persistence in recent practice. It is still occasionally manipulated to serve the needs of political systems. But any idealized pretensions have given way to more immediate if less lofty concerns. Like the military engineers who appropriated the form in the seventeenth and eighteenth centuries for their own convenience, so today the land developer/speculator has made a similar requisition. The plan still shows up in places widely separated in place and circumstances, but with rare exception it has been enlisted not to design shelter for a perfect urban society but to market land in a commercialized and imperfect world.

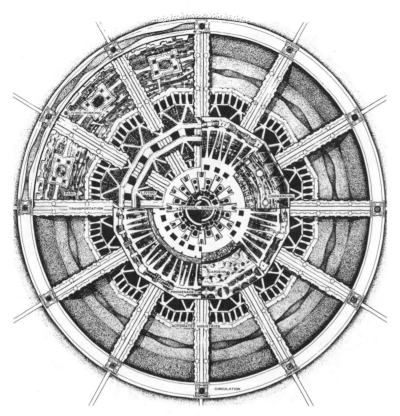

82. Soleri, plan of a circular city, 1969. Reprinted from Soleri, The City in the Image of Man, *by permission of the MIT Press, Cambridge, Mass. Copyright © 1969 by The Massachusetts Institute of Technology. All rights reserved.*

Nineteenth- and Twentieth-Century Circular City Applications

Requirements for new cities have always been specialized, responding to competitive border relationships, an expansion into open lands, or ritualistic observance of some cosmic or human ascendancy. For much of the world of the last two

centuries, these conditions have been insufficient to support strong new city activity. Where there has been such activity, the attractions of the circular city have been overshadowed by planning approaches more amenable to individual initiative and rapid urban commercialization.

In Europe, new cities of the nineteenth and twentieth centuries have been the creatures of specialized interests: large land developers, industry, or the state. The resulting products reflect the limitations of modern-day objectives, which tend more toward the creation of satellites to existing cities than of self-sufficient urban units. With few exceptions Europe in these last two centuries has failed to expand upon its previous distinguished history of planned circular cities. Occasional essays include Cabourg (c. 1860, made famous by Proust) and Stella-Plage (early 1900s), both French resort cities with strong radioconcentric plans centering on casinos (fig. 83). But their coastal locations result in semicircular forms in the manner of Bogoroditsk, without the latter's crisp polygonal separation of city from countryside. Neither of these specialized vacation centers does more than toy with planned circular city themes.

Mussolini's Italy would aim more ambitiously. The 140 square miles of malarial Pontine Marshes just to the south of Rome had defied reclamation for centuries. Theodoric and the popes had in their time tried to develop a drainage system, but always nature thwarted their efforts. Mussolini saw this as a highly visible opportunity for his regime to reinforce itself politically through good works—land and jobs for Italy's poverty-plagued people.

The fifteen years before the Second World War witnessed a great national effort to tame the marshes, establishing a foundation on which present-day progress has been built. Besides networks of canals, gates, and pumping stations, new roads and bridges, and the creation of new farmlands, Mussolini's plans also included the founding of a series of five new towns and fifteen villages. One of the towns, Latina (originally named Littoria), was planned in the circular and radial city tradition.[8]

Latina's plan, strongly reminiscent of Grammichele, was the design of an almost unknown architect, Oriolo Frezzoti, who also planned most of its principal public buildings. Construction began in June 1932, and six months later was sufficiently advanced for the town to be officially "inaugurated" on 18 December. Work proceeded day and night, urged onward by Mussolini, often on the site, who saw the project not only as a manifestation of the benefits he was bringing to Italy but also as evidence of Fascism's vitality and efficiency, a testimony presented to both the nation and the world.[9] It was all a part of his overall propaganda effort toward a national commitment to revitalize the country's rural foundations. At the same time it was a means for creating jobs, especially among unemployed veterans, freeing them from "urban nomadism."

As the first plots became ready, Mussolini appeared in person, chest bared, harvesting the corn, to show the only battles the regime intended to back; the success of his initiative encouraged him to push on with founding other "new cities," as they were greeted with approval everywhere, creating for the regime an unhoped-for image of peace, work and national harmony.[10] [Riccardo Mariani]

Latina's growth was planned incrementally, initially for a population of 5,000 but with planned expansions to 20,000 and then 50,000 inhabitants.[11] By the late 1930s, however, national focus had shifted elsewhere, and the reclamation program and its goals were further blighted by the war as Allied armies moved across the province following the Anzio beachhead landings. Though Latina was itself largely spared, its 1945 population had stagnated at 20,000.

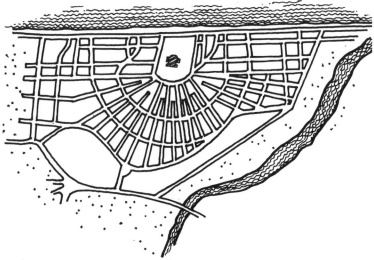

Cabourg

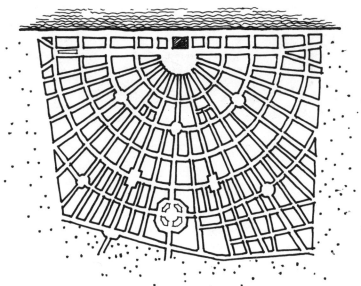

Stella-Plage

83. *Nineteenth-century French casino cities*

84. Plan of Latina, c. 1940

The city's postwar history is more promising. Reconstruction began fitfully in the province, but a largely uncoordinated, spontaneous small-scale industrialization together with a revival of agriculture and new tourism has brought vitality and expansion to both town and province. Latina is today a lively urban center of more than 70,000 residents and the capital of its province, though here too uncoordinated peripheral expansion has obscured any initial clarity of its original outline

(fig. 84). But time has softened the city's visual harshness; its street scenes reflect the historical development that one comes to expect of an Italian small town with an optimistic twentieth-century pace. Even today the focus remains the town square, the center of Latina's irregularly polygonal and radial plan.

The Mediterranean world of the early twentieth century offers another example of circular city lineage: Nahalal in Israel. Its binding ideological communalism and its function as a co-operative agricultural kibbutz (or *Moshav*) are both expressed by a sunburst plan (fig. 85). Designed in 1921 by the architect Richard Kauffman, it follows the same format as Chaux with an areal reach in the manner of Karlsruhe: an inner town center of community facilities and functions with a surrounding ring of housing (backed up to gardens at Chaux, agricultural fields at Nahalal). More open than Chaux, Nahalal's freestanding residences, yards, gardens, and outer fields are part of a closed economic and social system appropriately complemented by its plan (which may also imply a ringed defense against the external hostilities that still remain a sad reality for that land).

Also in the early twentieth century, the English, whose planning history had demonstrated such consistent indifference to circular city allures, were at last to succumb briefly. Perhaps the expansive self-confidence of Edwardian Britain contributed to an atmosphere that encouraged a certain extravagance of taste, the same imperial vision that was to linger on sufficiently to produce Lutyens' and Baker's multiradial though noncircular plan for New Delhi, India.

Whiteley Village, though infinitely more modest in ambitions, is cut from similar cloth. Its development came about through the generosity of a successful Yorkshire mercantilist whose will left provisions for the planning and construction of a retirement community. Such a community had roots in the English Cottage Homes movement as a derivative of the coun-

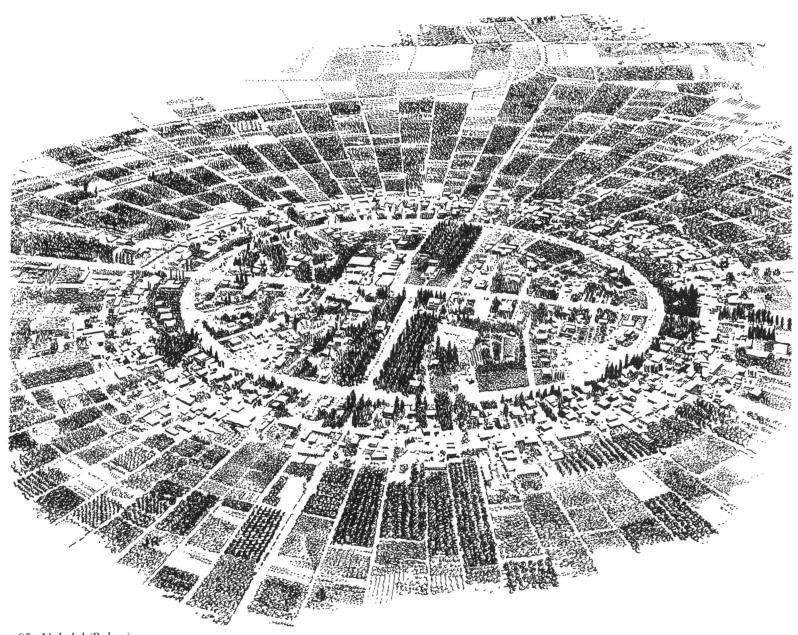

85. *Nahalal (Rohrer)*

try's traditional local almshouse. By the turn of the century, however, it had been translated into a more attractive environmental movement with the support of enlightened employers or philanthropists. The cottage was itself seen as a module more humanely scaled to those it housed and less institutionally intimidating. Whiteley Village picks up that theme but applies it with unexpected formalism.

Land was purchased in Surrey on a site to the southwest of London just beyond its metropolitan limits. There, on some 225 acres, the architect Frank Atkinson laid out an octagonal and radial plan that would be England's only ideal city adventure. Atkinson's plan had been chosen in 1912 from several submitted in a competition, so the design decision it represented, even if it was some caprice on the part of the architect, had also struck a responsive chord with the village's trustees (fig. 86). It radiates out from a circular central green beyond which are the curving blocks of housing enclosed within the peripheral octagonal street that largely limits the area of development. The remaining acreage is wooded or contains various support buildings, unexpectedly including the church and village hall. Given the ideal city model, one might have expected these would have been in or close to the central communal space.

The cottages, mostly single story, housed some 350 residents and were designed by various architects whose only restraint was that all be built with the same red brick. Besides the cottages, hall, and church, the village contains stores, post office, restaurant, and library. The results (mostly built from 1914 to 1921) were and remain a blending of English housing traditions and continental planning theory, pleasantly unified by substantial brick construction set in well-tended lawns and gardens ringed by wooded grounds that preserve the village's identity and reinforce its sense of community. Though late to the idiom, Whiteley Village is a specialized but sensible interpreta-

tion of the circular city that within the limits of its ambitions does justice to its lineage.[12]

In the United States, circular cities have been more ephemeral than those of the Old World. Except for some early eighteenth-century Spanish presidios in today's Texas and Louisiana that were never much more than polygonal-radial paper plans, urban design has relied mainly on spontaneous growth or the pragmatics of rectangular geometry.[13] With the nineteenth century and the rapid expansion of population into the western territories, the hundreds of resulting cities only rarely

86. *Plan of Whiteley Village*

indulged in the peculiarities of the circular plan. Instead, the standardization, simple principles, and unlimited potential for expansion of the orthogonal grid would dominate the plans of new cities. Concentrating on facile merchandising and rapid development, new city sponsors would be little attracted to a planning approach that suggested more than minimal constraints on the whims of the property owner or any potential pause in the swift exchange of land for cash. The absence of any particular affinity for formal ritual, the strong pragmatic personality of the people, their disinclination to subordinate private property rights to community standards, and the feverish pace of nineteenth-century urban expansion—all were calculated to discourage, even to suppress, planning adventures in the circular city idiom. The paucity of its employment here and the fate of those infrequent experiments with it confirm America's inhospitality to cities in the round. In such circumstances, the exceptions, because they are so rare, have an unearned increment of interest that transcends their otherwise comparatively modest achievement.

John Reps has traced an amusing example of this inhospitality in the history of Circleville, Ohio.[14] Its planner, Daniel Driesback, impressed by existing local remains of the work of the Indian Mound Builders, chose to combine their circular and square plan forms in his 1810 plan of the new city. They were worked into a polygonal inner core with radial streets surrounded by blocks laid out to form a strictly grid-planned periphery with no limits to future expansion. The central open space was occupied by an octagonal courthouse (could Driesbach have known that he was following Renaissance formulas?). But the awkwardness that the plan presented, especially in the corner triangles of transition between the inner circle and its surrounding rectangular frame, and the temptations of further land exploitation through replatting, resulted in a move by local people to revise the plan. So, through a succession of

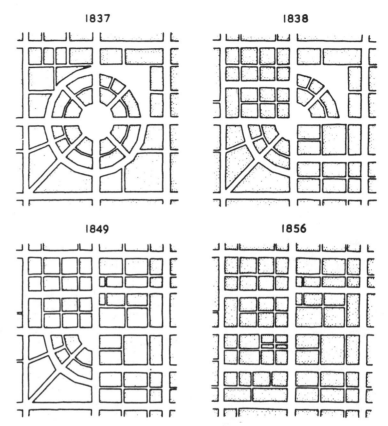

87. *The squaring of Circleville* (*Reps,* Making of Urban America). *Reprinted from "The Squaring of Circleville, Ohio: 1837–1856," in John W. Reps,* The Making of Urban America: A History of City Planning in the United States (*copyright © 1965 by Princeton University Press*). *Reprinted by permission of Princeton University Press.*

replats, by 1856 Circleville's distinctive core had entirely disappeared (fig. 87). As Reps wryly notes, "The squaring of Circleville had been accomplished."[15]

America's mid years of the nineteenth century were tempting ones for groups with their own distinctive and occasionally exotic brands of utopianism. The reputation (if not always the reality) of the American dream was openness to new ideas. This, combined with a generous supply of available land, encouraged all sorts of separatists both here and abroad to establish themselves here in communities where they could live out the peculiarities of their theories. Étienne Cabet had come to do just that in 1848 with an Icarian community which he established in Texas. Though neither this nor other Icarian communities in the United States were successful, they nevertheless lingered on until the late 1800s. But they were all engrossed in Cabet's social rather than his design theory. In fact, the record of most utopian experiments in this country followed similar lines; only rarely did they indulge in physical planning ambitions, being preoccupied with matters of social organization and interpersonal relationships. Occasionally a radial plan might be employed, but the creation of a circular city was likely to exceed by far the environmental goals of American utopians.

There was to be a brief theoretical circular hybrid out of a union of vegetarianism and phrenology. Both phenomena had achieved a considerable following by 1850; a leader of the former, Henry Stephen Clubb, was attracted to the ideas of a leading spokesman of the latter, Orson Fowler. Among Fowler's enthusiasms was the building of houses with octagonal plans, for reasons that evoke earlier efforts along similar lines:

But is the square form the best of all? Is the right-angle the best angle? . . . Nature's forms are mostly *spherical*. She makes ten thousand curvilineal to one square figure. Then why not apply her forms to houses? . . . Since, as already shown, a circle incloses more space for its surface, than any other form, of course the nearer spherical our houses, the more inside room for the outside wall, besides being more comfortable. . . . Of course the octagon, by approximating to the circle, incloses more space for its wall than the square, besides being more compact and available. . . .

FORM imbodies an important element of beauty. Yet some forms are constitutionally more beautiful than others. Of these the spherical is more beautiful than the angular, and the smooth and undulating than the rough and projecting. . . . And the more acute the angle, the less beautiful; but the more the angle approaches the circle, the more beautiful. Hence a square house is more beautiful than a triangular one, and an octagon or duodecagon than either. . . .

Since, then, the octagon form is more beautiful as well as capacious, and more consonant with the predominant or governing form of Nature—the spherical—it deserves consideration.[16]

Alberti could hardly have stated it more specifically.

Clubb was attracted to these ideas and sought to apply them in 1856 to a series of vegetarian villages he hoped to found in

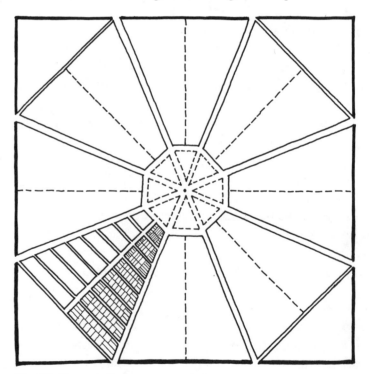

88. Clubb, *plan for an octagonal city*

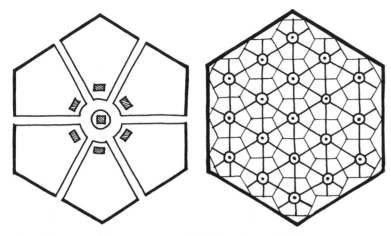

89. *Allen, plan for an octagonal block and city, 1873*

eastern Kansas which were to have octagonal plans (fig. 88). Even though his descriptive brochures were weighted toward the potentials that landowners in his octagonal agricultural villages could anticipate for denser (and more profitable) urban development, the informal union of vegetarianism and phrenology died without further issue.[17]

Another fleeting experiment with polygonal plans was the ideal city by J. Madison Allen. Its credentials in the literature of utopias were authenticated through publication in 1873 of its plan by Josiah Warren, who was a member of the Owenite colony of New Harmony, Indiana, and had himself been a founder of the anarchistic community of Modern Times, New York, as well as Utopia, Ohio. Hexagonal in outline, its plan suggested the web of a honeycomb, a city with no single center but rather nineteen of them, each the focus of its own group of six three-to-five-acre residential lots about a central circular open space and public building (fig. 89). Like Clubb's octagons, Allen's multiple hexagons failed to take the step from theory to reality.[18]

California, ever a destination for the eccentric if not the bizarre, has had a small cluster of adventures in circular city planning as yet another facet of its history of varied social and environmental experimentation. The earliest of the group, Corona (platted in 1886), was also known as "Circle City" because of its one-mile diameter circular "Grand Boulevard."* But its inner sanctum was entirely grid-planned. So also were its external agricultural areas, part of the same real estate development scheme, the farm plots slightly modified to suit an essentially orthogonal orientation with no overriding rationale. The city and its boulevard still exist as a unit in the eastward sprawl of the Los Angeles metropolitan area.[19]

Almondale, also in the Los Angeles region but to the north, has disappeared, the principal testimony to its past being its presence recorded on the Official Map of the County of Los Angeles of 1898. It had been founded in the early 1890s by a Chicago group inspired by the colonizing example of Horace Greeley of the *New York Tribune*. Organized with the support of the magazine *Farm, Field and Fireside*, it was based on the expectation of irrigation water for the growing of almond trees. But bankruptcy came before the water supply, and within three years its residents had left.[20] Almondale deserved better; its plan, superficially like Corona's, had two rings of circumferential streets about an inner city grid, with radials extending out from the outer ring to the limits of its section of the national grid† (fig. 90). Had it survived, it would have been a charming nineteenth-century reminder of the persistence of ideal city form.

---

* Its usefulness as a raceway was exploited in 1913 when it was the route for the first organized car race.

† The survey system of rectangular townships and sections for identifying all western lands. It was adopted by the Congressional Congress as the Land Ordinance of 1785.

90. *Plan of Almondale*

Not until the end of that century do we come to an American city with circular plan pretensions that not only was built but remains (though blighted) to the present day: Cotati, some forty miles north of San Francisco. Does the fact that it had no theoretical, philosophical, or other utopian ambitions account for its relative success in this otherwise frustrated record? The American reality has been that those idealistic communities that matched most clearly the economic and social characteristics of their conventional contemporaries were most likely to survive. Cotati's only unusual quality was its plan, but even this might not have endured, as the case of Circleville has already demonstrated. Perhaps the California social climate pro-

vided the residents of Cotati with that extra dimension of tolerance permitting them to live peacefully with the unconventional, including their city's plan.

Cotati (from the name of an Indian village named for its chief, Cotate) was first given official identity in a land grant dated 17 July 1844 in which Rancho Cotati was assigned to a Captain Juan Castaneda. A Texan of Mexican blood, he was a figure of prominence in the California of those days. However, failing to fulfill the legal requirements of the grant, he lost it. In 1847 Dr. Thomas S. Page arrived in the state and received the appointment of sheriff for the District of Sonoma. He applied for the Cotati lands in 1852, and the grant was made final by court action five years later; after final title clearance, Dr. Page was deeded 13,000 acres, which he used as a stock ranch.

There is some uncertainty as to who was actually responsible for the design of the town, whether the doctor or his six sons. The official plat, filed with Sonoma County on 7 June 1893, certifies one of the sons, Charles, as being president of the Cotati Company, the sponsoring corporation. What is entirely clear is that the hexagonal plan was happily coincident with the number of the doctor's sons, and each could therefore be remembered by a street named after him (fig. 91). Family sentiment and the merchandising of city land, rather than cosmology or philosophy, appear to have been the inspiration for the city's plan, which under the circumstances seems entirely appropriate. The balance of the original deed's acreage was either subdivided into small farms of five to twenty acres or retained by the Cotati Company for the cultivation of hay and grain. Most of the Pages then decamped for the attractions of San Francisco, leaving the company's affairs and the town to hired management.[21]

The Cotati that developed was a city of small frame houses and commercial buildings of no special achievements or visual

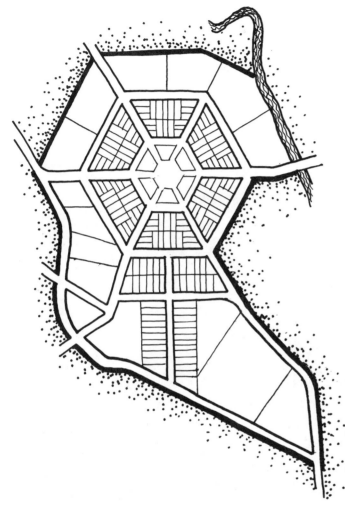

91. *Plan of Cotati*

distinction. The rather grand two-dimensional ambitions of its plan cannot be said to have been matched by its three-dimensional interpretation. Now that it is an incorporated city with the usual functions (including a planning commission), some effort is being made to "preserve the rural identity of Cotati,"

including zoning regulations and design review procedures. The town square, "the Plaza," now designated a National Historic Landmark, had been donated by the Pages as public open space; much of it is still sufficiently spacious with lawns and trees to create a pleasant park.

Conscious of their unusual city plan, Cotati residents like to refer to the city as the "Hub of Sonoma County," its radiating spokes of highways racing out into the surrounding region and to nearby (and grander) cities (fig. 92). The new freeway alignment for U.S. 101 provides easy access both north and south and has accelerated the pace of residential, commercial, and industrial growth in the valley. New developments now surround the original plan and cause one to wonder about the security of Cotati's "rural identity." But in spite of such limitations, its identity with the planned circular city tradition is the best this country has to offer.

California was to have a final experiment in egalitarian communal living that called for a colony to be laid out on the basis of a radioconcentric plan. Though it never went beyond the drawing stage, Llano del Rio's plan has an interesting continuity with the past. The site was one used earlier by Almondale, then abandoned, but the new group, unusually committed to a "unique and beautiful" environment and unaware of the earlier failure, chose it for the building of their Socialist agricultural and industrial community, their "white city." The administration of the colony was acknowledged by its residents to have had a considerably authoritarian style, which may account for the facility with which the colony's designers drew from circular city traditions. A preliminary plan (1915) was prepared by a Leonard A. Cooke with interesting overtones of Grammichele (fig. 93), but Ebenezer Howard was to be the inspiration for the colony's ultimate plan. Its designer, Alice Constance Austin, who was both planner and architect for Llano and a proponent of what she considered to be a neces-

92. *Cotati (Rohrer)*

sary authoritarianism in its development, appears to have drawn directly from Howard's diagram. But she ignored his warning about its diagrammatic intentions only, applying it literally to her plan for the city (fig. 94). Thus, there was a circular civic center of public buildings with open spaces and a surrounding ring of buildings to house commercial, religious, educational, and light industrial functions. The residential blocks, generously open with park areas, radiated out from the center and were outlined by regularly-spaced radial and circumferential streets. Llano also followed Howard's lead by requiring communal ownership of land and buildings. But all

94. *Austin, plan for Llano, c. 1916*

was abandoned when the residents in 1917 moved on to Louisiana.[22]

The more recent decades of the twentieth century have not seen the demise of the planned circular city; instead it continues with scattered applications to contemporary needs, both internationally and in the United States. Of course, the purposes for such cities have been secular and rational, with a certain residue of the authoritarianism of the past in the extent to which their residents have been expected to subordinate themselves to a set environmental cast. But there have been occa-

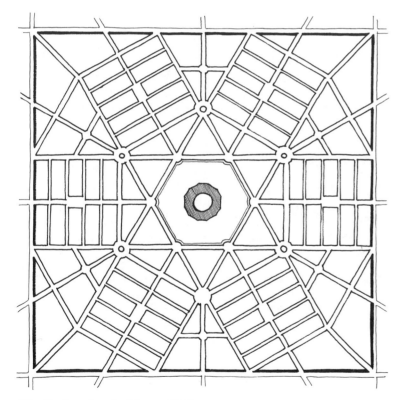

93. *Cooke, plan for Llano, 1915*

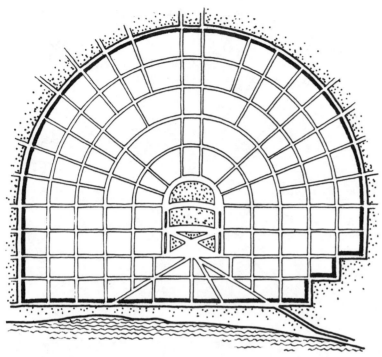

95. *Plan of Boa Vista*

sions when that has not been judged a deterrent or when the form has been applied in new ways to avoid such implications, even to enhance individuality within a community context.

Brazil, with the interesting precedents of its Bororo and Krahno Indian villages, has made a number of twentieth-century essays into the planned circular city idiom. Boa Vista, like Bogoroditsk a river city semicircular in plan, is in the northwest corner of the country on the banks of the River Branco, a tributary of the River Negro (fig. 95). A cattle-raising center, it had a population of 37,000 in 1972. Due west of Rio de Janeiro is another such effort, built in the 1960s at the site of Urubupunga as a community for 10,000 workers and their families during construction of a power station complex on the River Parana (fig. 96). The hope was that, once the work was finished, the city could continue as a normal urban center and help to populate the empty Brazilian interior, relieving concentrations on the coast. Like Pemberton's ideal city, this one was to have a model farm at its center and also introduce new settlements into open lands. But once construction ended, the residents hastened elsewhere, leaving the city to an ignominious fate, one half taken over by the army, the other half bulldozed away.[23]

One other Brazilian circular city adventure was never to be realized at all, but its intentions were splendid and deserve recalling. In 1946, the government determined a site for its new national capital, Brasilia, and by 1957 was reviewing the projects submitted in a national competition for its design. Among the twenty-five proposals was a remarkable plan submitted by the Roberto brothers, not one hexagonal unit but a cluster of seven of them! Though it was not to be Brasilia's new plan (Lucio Costa was the winner), it was generally considered to be a distinguished runner-up (fig. 97).

The rationale was one interestingly similar to Gloeden's: to design the city not as a single unit but in multiples, each a self-sufficient "urban unit" of 72,000 inhabitants with all the functions necessary for community life (figure 98). The forms were all the same, a hexagon with radials out from the center, an exact duplicate of Grammichele, though no acknowledgment of this coincidence has been found. The Roberto report says only that "the almost flat nature of the terrain made possible a fully rational layout. There was no justifiable purpose in introducing romantic irregularities or useless complications."[24] The brothers also felt that the population potential of Brazil and of the city was too explosive to tie it to any limits; the multicellular approach was intended to permit future expansion by additional urban units, avoiding the problems of living in a partially completed city, disrupting existing units, or los-

96. *View of Urubupunga* (*Moholy-Nagy*, Matrix of Man)

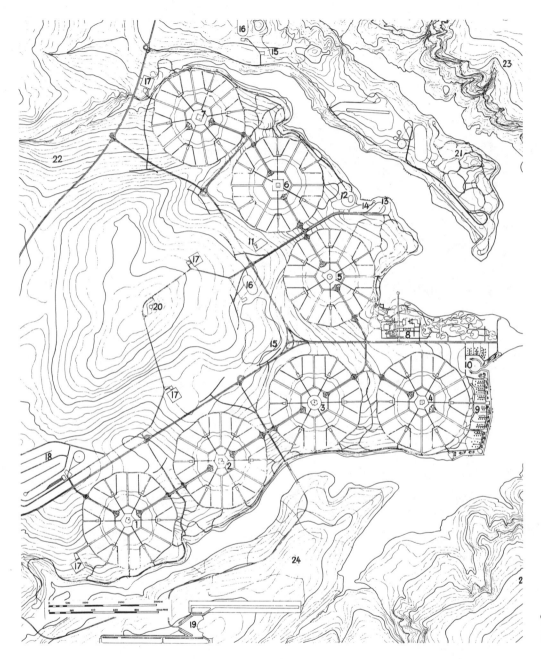

97. *Roberto plan for Brasilia*
(*Evenson,* Two Brazilian Capitals)

ing the sense of the city's formal structure and urban system through sprawl. Involved also in the multinuclear structure was the organization of the capital's functions, since each of the seven urban units would have at its core some specified group of offices and services. Thus, unit one was for regional administration, two for communications, three for finance, four for the arts, five for letters and science, six for welfare services, and seven for production agencies. The buildings necessary for housing these functions, together with those for shopping and recreation, would be located at the unit's central core from which the areas radiated out to where workers and their families lived. There was a Federal Park where some of the key agencies of government would be located, but total centralization was not planned, the urban units being expected to include those federal agencies appropriate to their focus.

Organization of the residential areas within an urban unit was by low and high density housing in neighborhoods of some 4,000 inhabitants supported by a full range of service facilities scaled to that population. Transportation was a major design determinant, emphasis being on easy walking distances and public transportation (including monorail transit and moving sidewalks, both above and below ground). Private cars would therefore be needed only for recreation or for trips beyond the urban unit. As the Roberto report summarized:

We have tried to design a Capital for a Nation that places the true values of human life above foolish exhibitionism or reckless mechanical complication. It is, we hope, a city for citizens, not for slaves or robots. There is no preoccupation to imitate other Capitals, as it seems more appropriate to take account of our own realities, and look to the future, rather than just copy the past.[25]

Nevertheless, the Roberto brothers at least in form copied the past more than they admitted.

These contemporary applications of the circular form in planning usage have completed its demythologizing. Ranked at one time as the essence of pure beauty and an expression of unity between earthly and cosmic systems, the circular form has been diminished in the twentieth century to accessory service. Given the history of the planned circular city, its modern-day circumstances are clearly reduced. At Sun City, an Arizona retirement community developed in 1960, the circle has not been used as a dominant theme but has been woven in and out of a generally undulating plan (fig. 99). No cosmic overtones here; the designers chose the circle as an aid in locating residents within easy walking distance of playgrounds and golf courses and to slow down traffic on the concentrically curving streets. The center, marked by Vitruvius for the placing of the temple, reserved by the Renaissance for a noble domed building, chosen by Baroque planners as the radiating point for a palace or fortress, is where Sun City developers have built shopping malls and parking lots, "a mandala of the consumer society."[26]

These last two centuries have not been without some interesting episodes attesting to the longevity of the planned circular city in the search for idealized urban expression. But technological and developmental pressures, together with the fragmentation of political and cultural directions and an economics of individualism, conspired against it. The squaring of Circleville was more than a quirkish episode in the life of a small Ohio town. It demonstrated in its day-by-day realities its own version of a fundamental contemporary ideal, the exploitation of land. To that end, orthogonal principles applied more handily than the introduced intricacies of the circle. Under such circumstances the peculiarities of a city in the round had

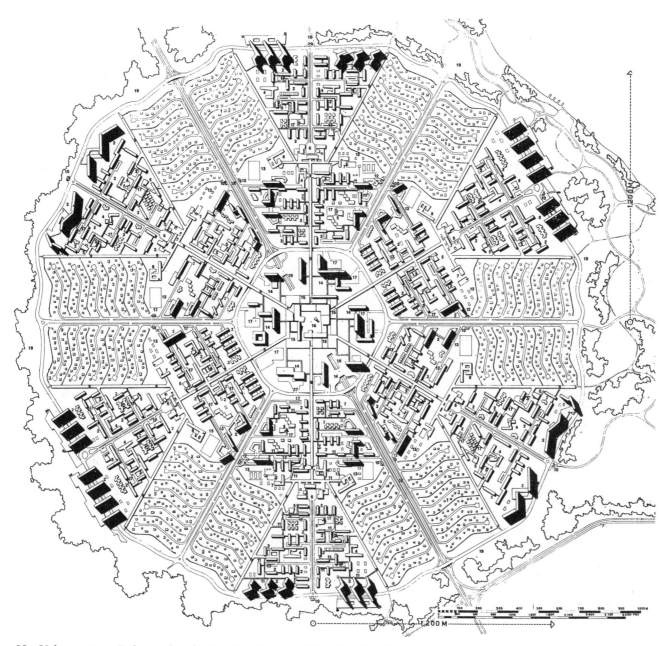

98. *Urban unit in Roberto plan for Brasilia* (Evenson, Two Brazilian Capitals)

to go—and they did. Only when the circular module was temporarily united with the remnants of authoritarianism or the merchandising of property did it survive theory to become practice. Despite its long and distinguished history as a planning form, the circle has today lost not only its mystique but even its identity, reduced in a recent appearance to the status of an anonymous handmaiden in the service of the affluent retired.

99. *Partial plan of Sun City*

VIII. A Postscript for Circular Cities

THERE ARE just so many permutations that the circle as an urban module permits, and most of them have been investigated at one time or another as the basis for the planned circular city. Some even reached reality, crystallized in cities that still impress the viewer by their evocative designs. They need not have all been a Palmanova or Neuf Brisach to remind us by their presence of the grand scale of thought and action necessary to inspire their construction. Even the remnants of Coevorden or the faulted frailties of Cotati sustain that sense of sharing in a formal vocabulary that is neither pedestrian nor mean. Gur's great sweep of its circular wall; the polygonal moated outline of Willemstad; the perimeters and radials of Nahalal; even the contrivances of Latina: all by their patterns are linked together as users of a centuries-old and distinguished urban language. What have changed, however, for cities in the round are the theories that inspired them. These conceptual roots, though drawing deeply from human aspirations, appear by their evolutionary trend to be nurtured by energies increasingly narrow and impoverished—the City of the Sun on one hand, Sun City on the other.

The earliest circular cities were expressions of continuity with the universe, the supernatural, the mystic. Through these cosmic cities, people had an identity with higher powers; as participants in a larger order, they felt a comforting reassurance in a world of mysterious uncertainties. The river valley civilizations of the Near East were the first to build such cities, and their experiments and speculations were carried forward into Western thought and experience. Platonic philosophy, Vitruvian postulates, and Augustine's City of God were all part of an ongoing intellectualization of the cosmic tradition that maintained itself sufficiently to reach new flowering in Renaissance Europe.

But this transposition through space and time resulted in important conceptual adjustments. The major environmental researchers of the Renaissance were intellectuals searching for perfect beauty, the perfect temple, the ideal city, and the formulas calculated to realize them. Causality rather than cosmology was their motivation. Intellectual powers displaced the powers of the supernatural, though in either case the circle continued to be judged the form closest to perfect beauty and to God.

But if the planned circular city was chosen by the Renaissance intellectual as most expressive of perfect beauty, it was also vulnerable to selection by others for other—and less spacious—notions of perfection. Cities in the round were attractive also to the Renaissance military engineer, and, as has been seen, not only was his exploitation of their forms and patterns an enthusiastic one but rarely was there a built Renaissance or Baroque circular city that was not to his designs. Indeed, for the Baroque centuries, the philosopher for the planned circular city had become the military engineer.

The past two centuries have included moments of theoretical respectability for the circular city concept, though in that time its secularization has become complete. Pemberton, Howard, Gloeden, and Wolf have each in their own way brought contemporary breadth to the concept of the well-designed city, and each employed the circle as a means for its achievement. Even though both Austin and the Roberto brothers were dealing with the reality of planning for actual cities, their plans for Llano and Brasilia identify with the same theoretical lineage and thus reinforce one's sense of its influence.

But most of the contemporary efforts of frustrated utopians, bombastic authoritarians, or land speculators have done little to give any reminiscent luster to the circular city. It has, rather, been buffeted by miscellaneous corruptions for purposes that, while not necessarily ignoble, rarely aim for grander concepts of form and function. Ours is an age, especially in the United States, given to thinking of land as an exploitable resource. Only when the circular module has been found to serve that purpose has it been employed—for the service of commercial rather than celestial values.

Are there any potentials for application of circular city principles to contemporary circumstances? There are some aspects of the tradition that imply a certain usefulness. At a mechanical level, the circular form is conveniently joined to the technology of the geodesic dome. Buckminster Fuller, that lively advocate of the dome's versatility for a variety of environmental uses, sees its controlled interior environment as a unique liberator. Envisioned by him as almost infinitely expansive, the dome's protective circular umbrella could encompass an entire city, creating a whole new approach to shelter with fascinating potentials for adjusting conventional expectations about environmental influences on human relationships.[1]

Similar considerations would be likely should the time come for the building of communities on the moon. The requirements there for a totally controlled environment and the efficiencies of the geodesic dome in plan, section, and technology would combine to recommend that the cosmic circular city be projected into the planetary system of its inspiration. In that event, observes Sibyl Moholy-Nagy, the "cosmic circle of the concentric city will have been closed."[2]

Less poetic but more immediate is the value of an understanding of circular city principles in dealing with the current frailties of our cities: their vulnerability to an undifferentiated sprawl with its structural, visual, and social consequences, and the fracturing of urban functions and human relationships. The early circular city was a reflection of an idealized cosmic order, and the patterns of future development were clearly established by the city's plan, based on principles of definition and containment. Within the limits prescribed by the plan, facilities and functions could be scaled with some assurance. The clarity of the circular perimeter and the ordered pattern of the internal arrangement (both in themselves deterrents to casual breaching and disruption) imposed constraints on the inhabitants but also provided the security and cohesiveness of a community of dignity, order, and comprehendable human scale.

Such urban achievements are not unworthy of modern consideration. Howard in his Garden City theory recognized them; his circular-plan diagram in effect said of the city, "this far and no farther." It established the structural, social, and economic parameters within which the city was built and people lived. This is a level of urban order that eludes our cities today and contributes to their frightful condition. Reform requires more than physical rearrangements, but urban life can be enhanced by built environments that work in harmony with human needs rather than against them.

In the history of efforts to chart the urban environment, the planned circular city has never been a major foundation for actual construction. Even in sixteenth- and seventeenth-century Europe when circumstances were the most promising for its fulfillment, such cities were a mere scattering in the dense patterning of city development. Perhaps this failure was inevitable: human activity, dynamic, spontaneous, varied, was never sufficiently understood by either theorists or builders when they sought to accommodate it in the rigidities of idealized cosmic forms. The ritual was too heavy, the arrangements too sanitized, the form too literal, too removed from the nature of life, to make more than an uneasy union between the planned circular city and the human processes it was to house. Those instances in which the circle was most conspicuously employed were accompanied by an authoritarianism having little or no need to recognize the permutations of human society. If they thought of it at all, the autocratic regimes felt as free to order people about as to arrange the streets and buildings of their cities' stellar plans. And as the impact of eighteenth-century enlightenment began to be felt, the attractions of those plans became increasingly inauspicious.

As for the twentieth-century neglect of the circular city, this may tell us as much about ourselves as it does of the city: the failure of heroic vision. Though there are drawbacks to the use of the circle as a planning device, its application in a coordinated approach to the laying out of a city is evidence of unusual daring for such a complex task. Today our attitude as urban artists is cautious, our direction uncertain, our expectations pale. The audacity of a planned circular city venture calls for a self-confidence, faith, and resources unmatched by what the twentieth century is willing to offer. Cut off from our primal associations, doubtful of universal truth, disappointed in earlier promises and those making them, we are understandably distrustful of formulas whose terms are phrased in ideal presumptions. Cities in the round require and suggest expectations disadvantaged by the nature of modern life.

Peter Smith notes our contemporary bias against concepts that elude the analytic process and the degree to which we give priority to processes of logic. Ours are secular and demythologizing times in which decision-making—such as the planning of cities—is little attracted to such indeterminant considerations as symbols and the meanings they can have for the modern person: "it may be difficult for the rational executives of the environmental business to accept that feedback from previous ages affects perception of the modern urban scene." But in the traditional village patterns of primitive societies, in the philosophic search for ideal environments, or in the planning for a modern-day capital city, the persistence of the circular form may indeed reflect "symbolic references that go right back to archetypal origins." [3]

So, for all of what may appear to be the failures of the planned circular city or our uses of it, it has *not* failed to survive. Its persistency, at least in Western practice, is one of its most engaging qualities. The signal may be a weak one, blurred by or subordinate to others. Nevertheless, in the cities described in this book we are dealing with evidence of a lingering and engrammic vocabulary of form whose meanings transcend the merely rational and instead make contact with needs that are emotional, subconscious, but no less relevant to the human condition.

The planned circular city at first glance seems an unlikely resource for dealing with the needs of the contemporary city and its people. Yet its recurring and varied applications through history suggest more than superficial connections with fundamental human emotions. These are the emotions that must be identified and understood if our planning is to produce urban environments harmonious with primal needs as found intrinsic in the tradition of cities in the round.

Notes

Chapter I

1. Carl G. Jung et al., *Man and His Symbols*, p. 55.
2. Peter F. Smith, "Symbolic Meaning in Contemporary Cities," *Ekistics* 39 (March 1975): 162.
3. Nader Ardalan and Laleh Bakhtiar, *The Sense of Unity*, p. 29.
4. Bruno Munari, *The Discovery of the Circle*, pp. 6, 28.
5. Barrie Biermann, "Indlu: The Domed Dwelling of the Zulu," in Paul Oliver, ed., *Shelter in Africa*, p. 98.
6. Ibid., p. 99.
7. Joseph Rykwert, *The Idea of a Town*, p. 171.
8. Douglas Fraser, *Village Planning in the Primitive World*, pp. 20–21.
9. J. F. Scott, *A History of Mathematics*, pp. 10, 44.
10. Jung, *Man and His Symbols*, pp. 240–41.
11. Munari, *The Discovery*, p. 5.
12. Jung, *Man and His Symbols*, p. 240.
13. Rudolf Koch, *The Book of Signs*.
14. José and Miriam Argüelles, *Mandala*, p. 12.
15. Ibid., p. 15.
16. Ardalan, *Sense of Unity*, p. 10.
17. Jung, *Man and His Symbols*, p. 243.
18. E. A. Gutkind, *Urban Development in Eastern Europe: Bulgaria, Romania, and the U.S.S.R.*, p. 147.
19. Yi-Fu Tuan, *Topophilia*, p. 37.
20. Ibid., p. 166.
21. Ibid., p. 167.
22. U Kan Hla, "Traditional Town Planning in Burma," *Journal of the Society of Architectural Historians* 37 (May 1978): 92–93.

Chapter II

1. Paul Wheatley, *The Pivot of the Four Quarters*, p. 225. He lists seven regions of primary urban generation: Mesopotamia, Egypt, the Indus Valley, North China Plain, Mesoamerica, central Andes, and the Yoruba territories of southwest Nigeria.
2. Pierre Lavedan and Jeanne Hugueney, *Histoire de l'urbanisme: antiquité*, p. 22.
3. Herodotus, *The History*, book 1, p. 39.
4. K. A. C. Creswell, *A Short Account of Early Muslim Architecture*, p. 172.
5. Sibyl Moholy-Nagy, *Matrix of Man*, p. 60.
6. Translated from Ernst Egli, *Geschichte des Städtebaues*, vol. 1, p. 264.
7. Gaston Wiet, *Baghdad*, p. 11.
8. Jacob Lassner, *The Topography of Baghdad in the Early Middle Ages*, p. 232.
9. Quoted in Wiet, *Baghdad*, p. 13.
10. Creswell, Wiet, and Lassner are all important sources for material on Baghdad.

Chapter III

1. Plato, *The Laws*, pp. 129–30.
2. E. A. Gutkind, *Urban Development in Southern Europe: Italy and Greece*, pp. 549–50.
3. Ibid., pp. 16–17.
4. Carl Jung et al., *Man and His Symbols*, pp. 242–43.

5. Gutkind, *Urban Development in Eastern Europe*, p. 147.
6. Vitruvius, *The Ten Books of Architecture*, p. 22.
7. Ibid., pp. 25–27.

Chapter IV

1. Otto von Simson, *The Gothic Cathedral*, p. 25.
2. Ibid., p. 21.
3. W. E. Garrett, "Mexico's Little Venice," *National Geographic* 133 (June 1968): 880.
4. Georg Gerster, *Grand Design*, pp. 103, 105.

Chapter V

1. Rudolf Wittkower, *Architectural Principles in the Age of Humanism*, p. 18.
2. Marie Louise Berneri, *Journey through Utopia*, p. 3.
3. Wittkower, *Architectural Principles*, p. 15.
4. Leone Battista Alberti, *Ten Books on Architecture*, p. 138.
5. Ibid., p. 72.
6. Ibid., p. 134.
7. Antonio di Piero Averlino (known as Filarete), *Treatise on Architecture*, vol. 1, p. 25.
8. Wittkower, *Architectural Principles*, pp. 9–10.
9. Gutkind, *Urban Development in Southern Europe*, p. 122.
10. Paul Zucker, *Town and Square*, p. 107.
11. Henry Morley, *Ideal Commonwealths*, pp. 141–42.
12. Gutkind, *Urban Development in Southern Europe*, p. 115.
13. Horst de la Croix, *Military Considerations in City Planning: Fortifications*, p. 50.
14. Lewis Mumford, *The City in History*, pp. 345–46.
15. Lavedan, *Histoire*, vol. 2, p. 84.
16. Croix, *Military Considerations*, p. 49.

17. E. A. Gutkind, *Urban Development in East-Central Europe: Poland, Czechoslovakia, and Hungary*, pp. 167–70, 295.
18. Gerald Burke, *The Making of Dutch Towns*, p. 117.
19. Gutkind, *Urban Development in Southern Europe*, p. 121.
20. *Toeristengids 1977 Willemstad*, p. 11.
21. Ibid., pp. 3–4.
22. Burke, *Making of Dutch Towns*, pp. 119–23; E. A. Gutkind, *Urban Development in Western Europe: The Netherlands and Great Britain*, p. 42.
23. E. A. Gutkind, *Urban Development in Western Europe: France and Belgium*, p. 103.
24. Gutkind, *Urban Development in Western Europe: The Netherlands and Great Britain*, p. 223.
25. Croix, *Military Considerations*, p. 51.
26. Ibid.
27. Maria Giuffrè, *Utopie urbane nella Sicilia del '700*, pp. 53–54.
28. Mario Morini, *Atlante di storia dell'urbanistica*, p. 188.
29. Croix, *Military Considerations*, pp. 51–52.
30. Ibid., p. 52.
31. Ibid., pp. 52, 54; A. Visentin and O. Piani, *Guida di Palmanova*, pp. 7, 9–18; Zucker, *Town and Square*, pp. 19, 22–23.

Chapter VI

1. Cecil Stewart, *A Prospect of Cities*, p. 110.
2. Translated from Giuffrè, *Utopie urbane*, p. 32.
3. E. A. Gutkind, *Urban Development in Western Europe: France and Belgium*, p. 87.
4. Frederick R. Hiorns, *Town-Building in History*, p. 196.
5. Translated from Giuffrè, *Utopie urbane*, pp. 32–33.
6. Gutkind, *Urban Development in Western Europe: France and Belgium*, p. 93.
7. Support for the foregoing comes from a number of sources, especially Horst de la Croix, *Military Considerations*; Giuffrè, *Utopie*

urbane; Gutkind, *Urban Development in Western Europe: France and Belgium;* and Mario Morini, *Atlante di storia.*

8. Yi-Fu Tuan, *Topophilia,* p. 73.

9. Gutkind, *Urban Development in Western Europe: France and Belgium,* p. 420.

10. Alphonse Halter, Roger Herrscher, and Jules Roth, *Neuf-Brisach,* p. 9.

11. Ibid., pp. 7–12, 29.

12. Ibid., pp. 62–63.

13. Translated from Giuffrè, *Utopie urbane,* p. 19.

14. Ibid., pp. 17–19.

15. Ibid., pp. 74–79.

16. Ibid., pp. 65–66.

17. Ibid., p. 38.

18. Ibid., p. 52.

19. Piera Busacca et al., *Programma di fabbricazione,* p. 14.

20. Ibid., p. 15.

21. Ibid., p. 16.

22. I am especially grateful for the generous assistance of church and city officials in Grammichele.

23. E. A. Gutkind, *Urban Development in Central Europe,* p. 300.

24. Gutkind, *Urban Development in East-Central Europe,* pp. 170, 270.

25. Iurii Alekseevich Egorov, *The Architectural Planning of St. Petersburg,* pp. xix–xx.

26. A. W. Bunin, *Geschichte des russischen Städtebaues bis zum 19. jahrhundert,* pp. 89–92.

27. Moholy-Nagy, *Matrix of Man,* p. 60.

28. Vlacheslav A. Shkvarikov, *Ocherk istorii planirovki . . . russkirkh gorodov,* p. 163.

29. Henrik Lilius, *Der Pekkatori in Raahe.*

30. Olli Kivinen, *Hamina,* p. 62, and Erkki Pitkänen, *Hamina,* pp. 5–6. I also wish to acknowledge the special assistance extended to me in my research on Hamina by Rainer Knapas, now on the faculty of the Department of History of the University of Helsinki.

31. Gutkind, *Urban Development in Western Europe: France and Belgium,* pp. 95–100; Pierre Lavedan, *Histoire de l'urbanisme: Renaissance et temps modernes,* p. 247; Helen Rosenau, *The Ideal City,* pp. 87–88; and Yvan Christ, *Ledoux.*

Chapter VII

1. Stewart, *A Prospect of Cities,* p. 112.

2. Étienne Cabet, *Voyage en Icarie;* and Berneri, *Journey through Utopia,* pp. 223–24.

3. Gutkind, *Urban Development in Western Europe: The Netherlands and Great Britain,* pp. 283–84. This is a quotation from Pemberton's *The Happy Colony* (1854).

4. Ibid., pp. 283–95; Rosenau, *The Ideal City,* p. 139; and Moholy-Nagy, *Matrix of Man,* pp. 74–75.

5. Ebenezer Howard, *Garden Cities of To-Morrow.*

6. Paul Wolf, *Wohnung und Siedlung.*

7. Paolo Soleri, *Arcology: The City in the Image of Man,* p. 31.

8. *Lazio,* pp. 552–53.

9. Riccardo Mariani, "Le 'città nuove' del periodo fascista," *Abitare,* October 1978, p. 82.

10. Ibid., p. 94.

11. Ibid., p. 84.

12. Martin S. Briggs, "The Whiteley Village," *Journal of the Royal Institute of Architects* 28: 524–26; Gillian Darley, *Villages of Vision,* pp. 125–27; Ian Nairn and Nikolaus Pevsner, revised by Bridget Cherry, *The Buildings of England: Surrey,* pp. 520–21.

13. John W. Reps, *Cities of the American West,* pp. 60–65.

14. Reps, *The Making of Urban America,* pp. 484–90, and "Urban Redevelopment in the Nineteenth Century: the Squaring of Circleville," *Journal of the Society of Architectural Historians* 14: 23–26.

15. Reps, *The Making of Urban America,* p. 490.

16. Orson S. Fowler, *The Octagon House, a Home for All,* pp. 82, 88.

17. Reps, *The Making of Urban America,* pp. 492, 496.

18. Dolores Hayden, *Seven American Utopias,* pp. 24, 37.

19. Gerster, *Grand Design*, p. 203; Reps, *The Making of Urban America*, p. 406.

20. Hayden, *Seven American Utopias*, p. 293.

21. Mrs. John Hahn, "Cotati," pp. 1–2.

22. Hayden, *Seven American Utopias*, pp. 293, 298–303.

23. Gerster, *Grand Design*, pp. 23–24; Moholy-Nagy, *Matrix of Man*, pp. 75–76.

24. Norma Evenson, *Two Brazilian Capitals*, p. 132.

25. Ibid., p. 129. I am greatly indebted to Professor Evenson for her invaluable study of Brazilian capitals with its inclusion of the material on the Roberto plan.

26. Gerster, *Grand Design*, p. 104.

Chapter VIII

1. James Meller, ed., *The Buckminster Fuller Reader*, p. 305.

2. Moholy-Nagy, *Matrix of Man*, pp. 79–80.

3. Smith, "Symbolic Meaning," pp. 159, 163.

Bibliography

Alberti, Leone Battista. *Ten Books on Architecture*. Translated by James Leoni and originally published in 1726. Reprint edition edited by Joseph Rykwert. London: Alec Tiranti Ltd., 1955.

Ardalan, Nader, and Laleh Bakhtiar. *The Sense of Unity*. Chicago: University of Chicago Press, 1973.

Argüelles, José and Miriam. *Mandala*. Berkeley: Shambhala, 1972.

Aristophanes. *The Birds*. Translated by Patric Dickinson. London: Oxford University Press, 1970.

Averlino, Antonio di Piero (known as Filarete). *Treatise on Architecture*. Translated with introduction and notes by John R. Spenvrt. Vol. 1. New Haven: Yale University Press, 1965.

Benevolo, Leonardo. *The History of the City*. Cambridge, Mass.: MIT Press, 1980.

Berneri, Marie Louise. *Journey through Utopia*. Boston: Beacon Press, 1950.

Biermann, Barrie. "Indlu: The Domed Dwelling of the Zulu," in Paul Oliver, ed., *Shelter in Africa*. New York: Praeger, 1971.

Blumenfeld, Hans. "Theory of City Form, Past and Present," *Journal of the Society of Architectural Historians*, (July–December 1949): 7–16.

Bogdanovíc, Bogdan. "Symbols in the City and the City as Symbol," *Ekistics* 39 (March 1975): 140–46.

Branch, Melville C. "An Illustration of Vitruvius," *Journal of the American Institute of Planners* 25 (February 1959): 40.

Briggs, Martin S. "The Whiteley Village." *Journal of the Royal Institute of Architects* 28 (30 July 1921): 524–26.

Bunin, A. W. *Geschichte des russischen Städtebaues bis zum 19. jahrhundert*. Berlin: Henschelverlag Kunst und Gesellschaft, 1961.

Burke, Gerald. *Towns in the Making*. New York: St. Martin's Press, 1971.

————. *The Making of Dutch Towns*. London: Cleaver-Hume Press, Ltd., 1956.

Busacca, Piera; Giovanni Campo; Franz Faro; and Rosario Salpietro. *Programma di fabbricazione*. Grammichele, Italy: Comune di Grammichele, n.d.

Cabet, Étienne. *Voyage en Icarie*. Clifton, N.J.: A. M. Kelley, 1973.

Campanella, Tommaso. *Civitas solis*. Included in Henry Morley, *Ideal Commonwealths*. New York: Colonial Press, 1901, pp. 141–79.

Cataneo, Pietro. *I quattro primi libri di architettura*, 1554. Reprint edition, Ridgewood, N.J.: Gregg Press, 1964.

Choay, Françoise. *The Modern City: Planning in the 19th Century*. Translated by Marguerite Hugo and George R. Collins. New York: George Braziller, 1969.

Christ, Yvan, *Ledoux*. Paris: Éditions du Minotaure, 1961.

Cornford, Francis Macdonald. *Plato's Cosmology. The Timaeus of Plato*, translated with running commentary. New York: Liberal Arts Press, 1957.

Creswell, K. A. C. *A Short Account of Early Muslim Architecture*. Harmondsworth, Middlesex: Penguin Books, 1958.

Croix, Horst de la. *Military Considerations in City Planning: Fortifications*. New York: George Braziller, 1972.

Darley, Gilliam, *Villages of Vision*. London: Architectural Press Ltd., 1975.

Dell'arte dei giardini inglesi. Milan, 1800.

De Marchi, Francesco. *Della architettura militare*. Brescia, 1599.

Dickinson, Robert E. *The Western European City*. London: Routledge & Kegan Paul Ltd., 1951.

Du Cerceau, Jacques-Androuet, the Elder. *Livre d'architecture*. Paris, 1559.

Egli, Ernst. *Geschichte des Städtebaues*. Erlenbach-Zurich: Eugen Entsch Verlag, 1962.

Egorov, Iurii Alekseevich. *The Architectural Planning of St. Petersburg*. Translated by Eric Kluhosch. Athens, Ohio: Ohio University Press, 1969.

Errard de Bar-le-Duc, Jean. *De la fortification.* 1604.

————. *La Fortification demontrée et reduicte en art par feu.* Paris, 1620.

Evenson, Norma. *Two Brazilian Capitals.* New Haven: Yale University Press, 1973.

Fougères, Gustave. *Mantinée et L'Arcadie orientale,* Paris: Ancienne Librairie Thorin et Fils, Librairie des Écoles Françaises d'Athenes et de Rome, 1898.

Fowler, Orson S. *The Octagon House, a Home for All,* 1853. Reprint edition, New York: Dover Publications, 1973.

Fraser, Douglas. *Village Planning in the Primitive World.* New York: George Braziller, 1968.

Gadol, Joan. *Leon Battista Alberti: Universal Man of the Early Renaissance.* Chicago: University of Chicago Press, 1969.

Galantay, Ervin Y. *New Towns: Antiquity to the Present.* New York: George Braziller, 1975.

Garrett, W. E. "Mexico's Little Venice," *National Geographic* 133 (June 1968): 876–88.

Genty, Pierre-Raymond. *Villes françaises.* Paris: Les Publications Filmées d'Art et d'Histoire, 1965.

Gerster, Georg. *Grand Design.* New York: Paddington Press, Ltd., 1976.

Giedion, Siegfried. *Space, Time and Architecture.* Cambridge, Mass.: Harvard University Press, 1967.

Giuffrè, Maria. *Utopie urbane nella Sicilia del '700.* Palermo: School of Architecture, 1966.

Gutkind, E. A. *International History of City Development.*
> Vol. 1, *Urban Development in Central Europe.* New York: Free Press of Glencoe, 1964.
> Vol. 4, *Urban Development in Southern Europe: Italy and Greece.* New York: Free Press, 1969.
> Vol. 5, *Urban Development in Western Europe: France and Belgium.* New York: Free Press, 1970.
> Vol. 6, *Urban Development in Western Europe: The Netherlands and Great Britain.* New York: Free Press, 1971.
> Vol. 7, *Urban Development in East-Central Europe: Poland, Czechoslovakia, and Hungary.* New York: Free Press, 1972.
> Vol. 8, *Urban Development in Eastern Europe: Bulgaria, Romania, and the U.S.S.R.* New York: Free Press, 1972.

Hahn, Mrs. John. "Cotati." Unpublished ms. revised 30 July 1971, in the Public Library, Santa Rosa, California.

Halter, Alphonse. *Histoire militaire de la place forte de Neuf-Brisach.* Strasbourg: Éditions P. H. Heitz, 1962.

Halter, Alphonse; Roger Herrscher; and Jules Roth. *Neuf-Brisach.* Colmar-Ingersheim, France: Editions S.A.E.P., 1972.

Handlin, Oscar, and John Burchard, eds. *The Historian and the City.* Cambridge, Mass.: MIT Press and Harvard University Press, 1963.

Havell, E. B. *The Ancient and Medieval Architecture of India: A Study of Indo-Aryan Civilisation.* London: John Murray, 1915.

Hayden, Dolores. *Seven American Utopias.* Cambridge, Mass.: MIT Press, 1976.

Herodotus. *The History.* Translated by George Rowlinson and edited by Manuel Komroff. New York: Tudor Publishing Co., 1928.

Hiorns, Frederick R. *Town-Building in History.* London: George G. Harrap & Co. Ltd., 1956.

Hla, U Kan. "Traditional Town Planning in Burma," *Journal of the Society of Architectural Historians* 37 (May 1978): 92–104.

Howard, Ebenezer. *Garden Cities of To-Morrow.* London: Faber and Faber Ltd., 1951.

Hughes, Quentin. *Military Architecture.* New York: St. Martin's Press, 1974.

Jellicoe, Geoffrey and Susan. *The Landscape of Man.* New York: Viking Press, 1975.

Jung, Carl, et al. *Man and His Symbols.* Garden City, N.Y.: Doubleday & Co., 1964.

Kasner, Edward, and James Newman. *Mathematics and the Imagination.* New York: Simon and Schuster, 1940.

Kitao, Timothy K. *Circle and Oval in the Square of Saint Peter's.* New York: New York University Press, 1974.

Kivinen, Olli. *Hamina.* Helsinki: Suomalaisen Kirjallisuuden Kirjapaino Oy, 1965.

Koch, Rudolf. *The Book of Signs.* New York: Dover Publications, n.d.

Lampl, Paul. *Cities and Planning in the Ancient Near East.* New York: George Braziller, 1968.

Lang, S. "The Ideal City." *The Architectural Review* 112 (August 1952): 91–101.

Lassner, Jacob. *The Topography of Baghdad in the Early Middle Ages.* Detroit: Wayne State University Press, 1970.

Lavedan, Pierre. *Histoire de l'urbanisme: époque contemporaine.* Paris: Henri Laurens, 1952.

———. *Histoire de l'urbanisme: Renaissance et temps modernes.* Paris: Henri Laurens, 1959.

———. *Les villes françaises.* Paris: Éditions Vincent, Freal & Cie., n.d.

Lavedan, Pierre, and Jeanne Hugueney. *Histoire de l'urbanisme: antiquité.* Paris: Henri Laurens, 1966.

———. *L'Urbanisme au Moyen-Âge.* Paris: Arts et Métiers Graphiques, 1974.

Lazio. Milano: Touring Club Italiano, 1964.

Lilius, Henrik. *Der Pekkatori in Raahe.* Helsinki: Oy Weilin & Goos AB, 1967.

Maggi, Girolamo, and Iacomo F. Castriotto. *Della fortificazione delle città.* Venice, 1564.

Mariani, Riccardo. "Le 'città nuove' del periodo fascista," *Abitare,* no. 168 of no. 21 nuova serie (October 1978), pp. 76–91, 94–95.

Marks, Robert W. *The Dymaxion World of Buckminster Fuller.* New York: Reinhold Publishing Corporation, 1960.

Matthews, W. H. *Mazes and Labyrinths: Their History and Development.* New York: Dover Publications, 1970.

Meller, James, ed. *The Buckminister Fuller Reader.* Harmondsworth, Middlesex: Penguin Books Ltd., 1972.

Moholy-Nagy, Sibyl. *Matrix of Man.* New York: Praeger, 1968.

Morini, Mario. *Atlante di storia dell'urbanistica.* Milan: Ulrico Hoepli, 1963.

Morris, A. E. J. *History of Urban Form.* New York: John Wiley & Sons, 1974.

Mumford, Lewis. *The City in History.* New York: Harcourt, Brace & World, 1961.

Munari, Bruno. *The Discovery of the Circle.* New York: George Wittenborn, n.d.

Nairn, Ian, and Nikolaus Pevsner, revised by Bridget Cherry. *The Buildings of England: Surrey.* Harmondsworth, Middlesex: Penguin Books Ltd., 1971.

Oliver, Paul, ed. *Shelter in Africa.* New York: Praeger, 1971.

Patte, Pierre. *Mémoires sur les objets les plus importans de l'architecture.* 1769.

Perret, Jacques. *Des fortifications et artifices d'architecture et perspective.* Paris, 1601.

Pitkänen, Erkki. *Hamina.* Helsinki: Suomalaisen Kirjallisuuden Kirjapaino Oy, 1966.

Plato. *The Laws.* Translated by A. E. Taylor. London: J. M. Dent & Sons Ltd., 1960.

Reed, Anna M. "Cotati Past and Present," *The Northern Crown* 5 (November 1911): 1–5.

Reps, John W. *Cities of the American West.* Princeton, N.J.: Princeton University Press, 1979.

———. *The Making of Urban America.* Princeton, N.J.: Princeton University Press, 1965.

———. "Urban Redevelopment in the Nineteenth Century: The Squaring of Circleville." *Journal of the Society of Architectural Historians* 14 (December 1955): 23–26.

Rimpler, George. *Kriegs-Baukunst.* Frankfurt, 1671.

Rosenau, Helen. "Historical Aspects of the Vitruvian Tradition in Town Planning." *Royal Institute of British Architects Journal* 62 (October 1955): 481–87.

———. *The Ideal City.* London: Routledge and Kegan Paul Ltd., 1959.

Rykwert, Joseph. *The Idea of a Town.* Princeton, N.J.: Princeton University Press, 1976.

Sardi, Pietro. *Corno dogale dell'architettura militare.* Venice, 1639.

———. *Corona imperiale dell'architettura militare.* Venice, 1617.

Scamozzi, Vincenzo. *L'idea della architettura universale.* Venice, 1615.

Schäfer, Wilhelm (known also as Dilich). *Peribologia oder Bericht von Vestungs Gebauden.* Frankfurt, 1640.

Schmidt, Erich F. *Flights over Ancient Cities of Iran.* Chicago: University of Chicago Press, 1940.

Scofield, John. "Israel, Land of Promise." *National Geographic* 127 (March 1965): 394–434.

Scott, J. F. *A History of Mathematics.* London: Taylor & Francis Ltd., 1969.

Serlio, Sebastiano. *Tutte l'opere d'architettura et prospectiva.* Venice, 1619.

Shkvarikov, Vlacheslav A. *Gradostroitel'stvo*. Moscow: Academy of Architecture, 1945.

———. *Ocherk istorii planirovki . . . russkirkh gorodov*. Moscow: State Publisher, Literature on Construction and Architecture, 1954.

Simson, Otto von. *The Gothic Cathedral*. New York: Pantheon Books, 1956.

Smith, Peter F. "Symbolic Meaning in Contemporary Cities." *Ekistics* 39 (March 1975): 159–64.

Soleri, Paolo. *Arcology: The City in the Image of Man*. Cambridge, Mass: MIT Press, 1969.

Speckle (or Speklin), Daniel. *Architectura von Vestungen*. Strassburg: B. Jobin, 1589.

Stewart, Cecil. *A Prospect of Cities*. London: Longmans, Green and Co., 1952.

Storm, Hyemeyohsts. *Seven Arrows*. New York: Ballantine Books, 1972.

Sturm, L. Christoph. *Architectura civilis-militaris*. Augsburg, 1719.

Toeristengids 1977 Willemstad. Willemstad: Stadhuis, 1977.

Tuan, Yi-Fu. *Topophilia*. Englewood Cliffs, N.J.: Prentice-Hall, 1974.

Vauban, Sébastien le Prestre de. *Essais sur la fortification*. Paris, 1739.

———. *Manière de fortifier*. Amsterdam, 1689.

———. *Projet d'une dîme royale*. 1707.

Visentin, A., and O. Piani. *Guida di Palmanova*. Palmanova, Italy: Cartografica Visentin, 1976.

Vitruvius. *The Ten Books on Architecture*. Translated by Morris Hicky Morgan. New York: Dover Publications, 1960.

Volwahsen, Andreas. *Living Architecture: Indian*. New York: Grosset & Dunlap, 1969.

Weitz, Raanan. "Integrative Planning for Israel's Rural Cooperatives (Moshavim): A New Model," *Kidma* (Israel Journal of Development), no. 6/1975, pp. 3–11.

Wheatley, Paul. *The Pivot of the Four Quarters*. Chicago: Aldine Publishing Co., 1971.

Whittick, Arnold, ed. *Encyclopedia of Urban Planning*. New York: McGraw-Hill Book Co., 1974.

Wickberg, Nils Erik. *Finnish Architecture*. Helsinki: Otava Publishing Co., 1959.

Wiet, Gaston. *Baghdad*. Norman, Oklahoma: University of Oklahoma Press, 1971.

Wittkower, Rudolf. *Architectural Principles in the Age of Humanism*. London: Warburg Institute, University of London, 1949.

Wolf, Paul. *Wohnung und Siedlung*. Berlin: Verlag Ernst Wasmuth A.-G., 1926.

Wu, Nelson I. *Chinese and Indian Architecture*. New York: George Braziller, 1963.

Zucker, Paul. *Town and Square*. New York: Columbia University Press, 1959.

Index

Alberti, Leone Battista: city planning theories of, 36, 50

Allen, J. Madison: ideal city of, 115

Al-Mansur, Caliph: and new capital of Baghdad, 18

Almondale, California, 115, 117

Arabs: environmental arts of, 17–18

Arcology. See Soleri, Paolo

Army: role in Baroque life, 62; convenience of circular city for, 64

Assyrians: and "city" bas-relief, 14

Atkinson, Frank, 112

Atlantis: Plato's description of, 21–22

Austin, Alice Constance, 117, 119

Avola, Sicily, 84

Baghdad, 18–20, 22

Baroque society, 62, 64, 100; subverts ideal city, 61; and city designers' preference for grid plan, 66; preoccupied with defense and ritual, 100; overthrown at end of eighteenth century, 100. See also German Baroque theorists; Russia

Boa Vista, Brazil, 120

Bogoroditsk, USSR, 94, 108, 120

Bram, France, 26

Brasilia, Brazil, 120, 122, 127; Roberto brothers' plan for, 120, 123

Brazil: primitive circular settlements in, 4–5; twentieth-century circular cities of, 120

Brosse, Salomon de, 76

Cabet, Étienne: his city of Icaria, 102; in Texas, 114

Cabourg, France, 108

Campanella, Tommaso, 41–42

Cardo and decumanus: relevance to Roman city planning, 23

Cataneo, Pietro di Giacomo: his pattern book of city plans, 39; importance of fortifications for, 39–41

Cathedral, medieval: and Augustinian geometry, 28

Charleroi, France, 71, 77

Charles V, King of Spain: and circular cities, 45–46; bias toward fortress cities, 46

Chaux, France, 98–100; similarities with Nahalal, 110

Cheyenne Indians: tribal assemblies, 5

Cincirli. See Zincirli

Circle: as symbolic language, 3, 6, 7; in natural world, 3–4; in human actions, 4; for shaping human environment, 4, 9–10; ancient fascination with, 5–6; according to Jungians, 6; and mathematics, 6; and Stonehenge, 6; and divine, 6; in written language, 6; for religious, mythic, magic purposes, 6–7; use by medieval church, 7; contrast between uses in East and West, 11; as inspiration for Renaissance ideal city, 32, 36; doubts about its perfect order, 73–74; loses its mystique, 122–25; persistence as plan form, 128

Circle City, California. See Corona, California

Circleville, Ohio, 113, 123

Circular churches: Vitruvian influences on, 34–35

Circular city: in symbolic language, 3; in urban history, 3; in Western tradition, 3, 128; Zulu, 4; confined to West, 12; with radial plan, 13; as ritual center, 13; in ancient Near East, 13, 14, 126; practicality of, 13, 20; in Classical world, 21, 25; Roman thoughts on, 23–24; medieval unplanned, 26; Renaissance enthusiasm for, 31, 36; rarity of construction, 45, 127–28; and authoritarianism, 64, 128; convenience for army, 64; neglect or indifference toward, 93, 107, 110, 128; Russian variations of, 94; used for today's

purposes, 102, 107–8, 123, 125; used by Howard, 105; in United States, 112–13, 127; contemporary potentials of, 127, 128. See also Gloeden, Ernst; Renaissance circular city; Wolf, Paul

Circular villages, 4, 5

Cities: Burmese planning of, 11–12; Chinese planning of, 11; Indian planning of, 11; Sumerian, 14; Roman planning of, 23–24; symbolism of medieval, 26; planned medieval, 28; Russian, 90–92, 93

City defense: central Baroque preoccupation with, 64

City of God (Civitas Dei), 10, 26, 126. See also Cosmic city

Clubb, Henry Stephen: vegetarian villages of, 114–15

Coevorden, Netherlands, 52–53, 126

Cooke, Leonard A. See Llano del Rio

Copernican revolution: displaces Ptolemaic metaphysics, 31

Corona, California, 115

Cosmic city: in East and West, 11. See also City of God

Cotati, California, 116–17, 126

Ctesiphon, Iraq, 15–16, 18

Dante: familiar with Classical learning, 28; Commedia of, 28

Darabjerd, Iran, 16

Defense: as planning theme, 64

Dilich (Wilhelm Schäfer): influence of Italians on, 68

Driesback, Daniel. See Circleville, Ohio

Dürer, Albrecht: ideal city of, 54, 55

Eastern world: circular symbolism in, 7
Ecbatana, 22; described by Herodotus, 15; recalled by Campanella, 41
Egypt: hieroglyphics for "city," 10, 13
Eighteenth-century romanticism, 74–75
Eketorp, Sweden, 26
England: indifferent to ideal cities, 55–56
English Cottage Homes movement, 110, 112
Errard de Bar-le-Duc, Jean: ideal cities of, 70
Etruscans: contribute to Roman practices, 23

Filarete (Antonio Averulino): ideal city of, 36–37; his debt to Alberti, 37; subsequent influence of, 37, 41, 48
Finland: remote from ideal city thought, 94; orthogonal cities of seventeenth century, 96. See also Hamina, Finland
Fortifications: preoccupation with, 64; Baroque city dominated by, 66; French designs for, 70; Vauban's designs for, 70, 71
Fortress: ideal city as, 39, 44
Fowler, Orson, 114
France: tentative ideal city efforts, 53, 54
Freudenstadt, Germany: as ideal city experiment, 55

Garden City. See Howard, Ebenezer
Geodesic dome, 127
German Baroque theorists, 68
Germany: and ideal city activity, 54, 55
Giocondo, Fra Giovanni: three-dimensional ideal city of, 39
Gloeden, Ernst, 105–6
Grammichele, Sicily, 84–88
Greeks: aware of circular city concepts, 21; urban colonization policy of, 21; indifferent to circular city, 22
Greeley, Horace. See Almondale, California
Grid plans. See Orthogonal plans
Gur (Firuzabad), Iran, 16–17, 18, 19, 21

Hamadan, Iran: site of ancient Ecbatana, 15
Hamina, Finland, 96–98
Happy Colony, 103; influence on Howard, 103

Henrichemont, France, 76
Herodotus, 20; describes Ecbatana, 15, 22; recalled by Campanella, 41
Hieroglyphics, Egyptian: symbol for "city," 10, 13
Hittites: and city of Zincirli, 14
Howard, Ebenezer, 103–5, 126; influenced by Pemberton, 103; his Garden City theory, 105, 106, 126, 127; as inspiration for Llano del Rio, 117, 119
Hungarian court: Renaissance enthusiasm of, 48

Icaria. See Cabet, Étienne
Ideal city: Jerusalem as, 26; of the medieval world, 26; in Renaissance, 32; and ideal form theory, 35–36; Scamozzi's view of, 41; appropriated by military engineers, 44–45, 61; and preoccupation with planimetrics, 59; and neglect of social concerns, 59, 61; subsumed by Baroque values, 61, 64; Italian difficulties with construction of, 81; in Sicily, 81–83; and nineteenth- and twentieth-century pragmatism, 102. See also Dilich; Errard de Bar-le-Duc, Jean; Filarete; Perret, Jacques; Rimpler, George; Speckle, Daniel; Sturm, Christoph
Ideal city theory: of Plato, 22; exploited by military engineers, 44–45; reappears in eighteenth century, 73; attractive to Sicilian aristocrats, 83; neglected by Baroque society, 100; Howard's employment of, 105. See also Alberti, Leone Battista; Ledoux, Claude-Nicolas; Patte, Pierre
Ideal form theories, 34–36
Industrial Revolution, 73
Industrial society: planning cities for, 98, 100, 103, 105

Jerusalem: as ideal city, 26
Jung, Karl, 3; and followers, 6, 10, 19

Karlsruhe, Germany, 85, 88–89; radioconcentric plan of, 68; as synthesis of Baroque attitudes, 88
Kauffman, Richard, 110
Krahno Indians: circular villages of, 5

Landscape: English revolution in, 75
Language, written: and the circle, 6
Latina (originally Littoria), Italy, 109–10
Leblond, Jean Baptiste Alexandre: St. Petersburg plan of, 93
Ledoux, Claude-Nicolas: anticipates Garden City, 73; ideal city theories of, 73; as visionary architect, 98; plan for Chaux of, 98–100
Leopoldov, Czechoslovakia, 88
Literature: and Renaissance ideal city theory, 32; and military biases of Baroque urban theorists, 66
Littoria, Italy. See Latina, Italy
Llano del Rio, California, 117, 119, 127; influenced by Howard, 117, 119
Longwy, France, 77
Louis XIV, 64, 70, 78; paradigm of Baroque monarch, 62; and Neuf Brisach, 78, 81

Mandala, 8–10; plan for Rome based on, 24
Mantinea, Greece, 22–23
Marienbourg, Belgium: Vitruvian plan of, 46
Martini, Francesco di Giorgio: ideal city plans of, 37–39
Mathematics: important to St. Augustine, 27
Mato Grosso, Brazil: Bororo planned villages, 4
Medieval thought: as bridge to Renaissance, 30
Mexcaltitán, Mexico, 28–30; ancestral home of Aztecs, 29
Military applications: ideal city and, 39
Military concerns: as central preoccupation, 66
Military engineer: exploits ideal city, 44–45; planning role of, 64; dominates urban design, 66; adapts Vitruvius, 66; French, 70
Monarchy: ability to plan extravagantly, 62, 64; social centralism of, 62
Montaigu, Belgium. See Scherpenheuvel, Belgium
Mussolini: and Pontine Marsh program, 108–9; involved in Latina, 109

Nahalal, Israel, 110
Neo-Platonism: and medieval thought, 25; and St. Augustine, 28; contributes to Renaissance via medieval scholars, 34

Netherlands: struggles for independence, 48; makes pragmatic use of circular cities, 48–50. *See also* Coevorden, Netherlands; Willemstad, Netherlands

Neuf Brisach, 73, 126; Vauban's orthogonal plan for, 78; construction of, 81; settlement of, 81; modern history, 81

Nimrud: bas-relief from Assurbanipal's palace at, 14

Nördlingen, Germany, 26

Northern Europe: impact of ideal city theories on, 53

Nové Zámky, Czechoslovakia, 48

Orthogonal cities: in seventeenth-century Finland, 96

Orthogonal plans: Vauban's preference for, 71, 73; United States reliance on, 112; LeCorbusier's and Wright's commitment to, 107

Palmanova, 56–59, 68, 96, 126; designers for, 56–57; and Renaissance ideal city inspiration, 57; construction progress, 58–59; military history, 59; modern history, 59

Patte, Pierre: ideal city theories of, 73

Pemberton, Robert, 103, 120, 126; influence on Howard, 103

Perfect beauty: Renaissance search for, 34, 35, 126

Perret, Jacques, 76; ideal cities of, 68–70

Perspective, mechanical: a Renaissance enthusiasm, 32

Peter the Great: impact on urban history, 90

Philippeville, Belgium, 46–48

Plato, 126; describes urban model in *Laws*, 21; his theory of ideal city, 22; and Renaissance ideal city, 32, 34; *Timaeus* recalled by Campanella, 41

Plutarch: describes Rome, 24

Pontine Marshes: Mussolini's plan for, 108–9

Prince of Butera, Carlo Maria Carafa Branciforte, 85

Ptolemaic metaphysics: and Copernican revolution, 31

Queen Victoria, colony of: as Pemberton's Happy Colony, 103; similarities between its plan and Howard's Garden City diagrams, 103, 105

Radial street plan: supplanted by Baroque grid, 66

Renaissance: search for perfect beauty, 31, 34, 35, 126; importance of Classical arts and learning in, 31; scale of values, 31-32, 61; urban theorists of, 32; importance of Vitruvian theory in, 34

Renaissance circular city: limits on resources to build, 45; theories attract Sicilian aristocrats, 83; appropriated by military engineers, 126. *See also* Circular city

Rimpler, George: ideal city of, 68

Roberto brothers. *See* Brasilia, Brazil

Rocroi, France, 54

Rome, Italy, 24; Etruscan contributions to, 23

Russia: Baroque planning in, 88, 90, 92, 93

Russian cities: history of, 90–92; as instruments of governmental policy, 90, 92; located on rivers, 93–94; and variations on circular city themes, 94

Saarlouis, France, 71, 78

St. Augustine, 25, 26–28; uses circle, 7; his City of God, 26; writings of, 26–28; importance of mathematics to, 27; uses numerical and musical ratios, 27; and neo-Platonism, 28; and medieval cathedral, 28. *See also* City of God

St. Petersburg: Leblond's plan for, 92–93

Santo Stefano di Camastra, Sicily, 83–84

Sardi, Pietro: circular city of, 67

Scamozzi, Vincenzo: ideal city of, 41; and Palmanova, 56, 58

Schäfer, Wilhelm. *See* Dilich

Scherpenheuvel (Montaigu), Belgium, 75–76

Sforzinda: Filarete's ideal city, 37

Sharawadji, 75

Soleri, Paolo, 106–7

Speckle, Daniel (or Speklin): ideal city of, 42, 68; and social concerns, 43–44; and Italian inspiration, 54

Stella-Plage, France, 108

Stonehenge, 6

Sturm, Christoph: ideal city plan of, 68

Sumerian cities, 14

Sun City, Arizona, 123, 126

Symbolic language, 3

Symbolism in medieval cities, 26

Symbols: significance of, 3, 128

Theorists, Baroque: military biases of, 66; and quality of life, 67

Theory, ideal city. *See* Ideal city theory

Theory of beauty, Renaissance, 31

Utopianism in America, 113–14

Vauban, Sébastien le Prestre de: his concern for people, 64, 70; as Louis XIV's premier military engineer, 70; his preference for orthogonal plans, 71, 77; his preoccupation with military engineering, 71

Vegetarians. *See* Clubb, Henry Stephen

Venice: and Palmanova, 56

Versailles, France, 83, 85

Villefranche-sur-Meuse, France, 54, 76

Vitry-le-François, France, 53–54

Vitruvius (Marcus Vitruvius Pollio), 24, 25, 36, 46, 81, 122, 126; city planning theories of, 24–25; influences Renaissance urban theory, 25; and Renaissance ideal city, 32–34; uses human figure as design guide, 34; continuing interest in, 66; adapted by military engineers, 66

Warfare: affects city design, 64

Whiteley Village, England, 112

Willemstad, Netherlands, 50–52, 126

Wolf, Paul: circular city of, 106–7, 126

Written language and circle, 10

Yin and yang disk, 7

Zendjirli. *See* Zincirli

Zincirli, 14

Zulu cities. *See* Circular city

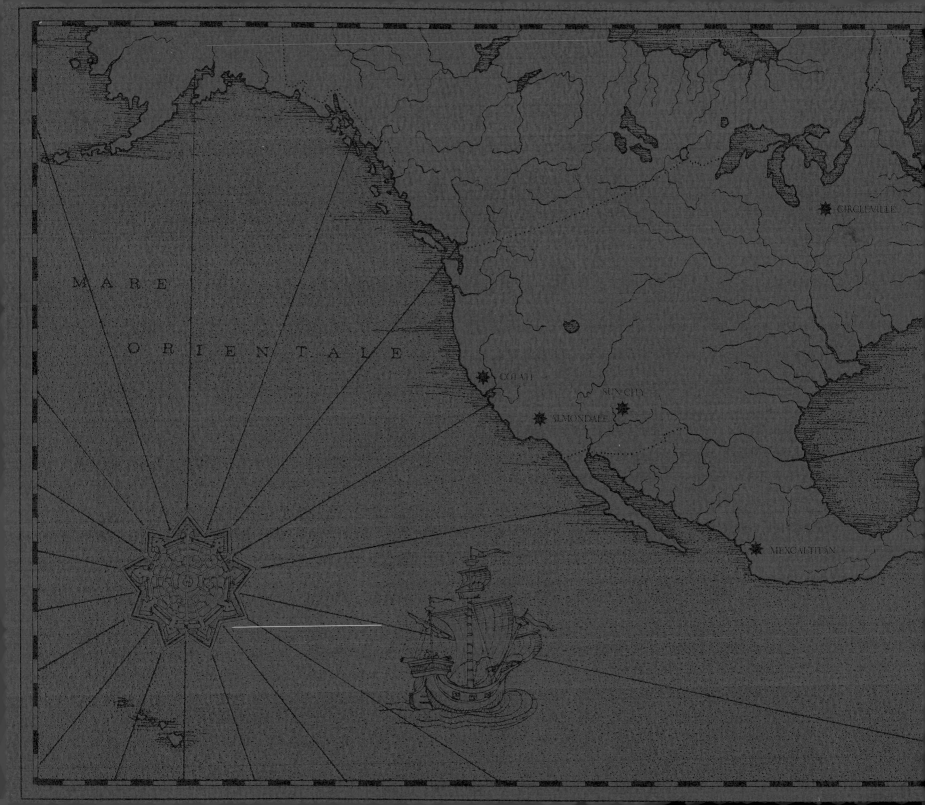